DENIED ACCESS

by David Chick

Written with Jed Novick

Indepenpress

Copyright © David Chick 2006
Written with Jed Novick

All rights reserved.
No part of this publication may be reproduced, stored in or
introduced into a retrieval system, or transmitted, in any form,
or by any means (electronic, mechanical, photocopying,
recording or otherwise) without the prior written
permission of the publisher

*The opinions made in this book are the views of the author and
do not reflect the opinions of the publishing company.*

*Some names have been changed in an effort to protect the
identity of those concerned.*

ISBN 1-905203-713

First published in Great Britain in 2006 by

Indepenpress Publishing
Pen Press Publishers Ltd
39 Chesham Road
Brighton
East Sussex BN2 1NB

A catalogue record for this book is available from
the British Library

Printed and bound in England

Cover design by Jacqueline Abromeit

**Dedicated to the two most important
girls in my life**

My darling daughter, for being the beautiful daughter
she is, her trust and unfailing love towards me.

Gemma, my fiancée, for her understanding, help, love
and support throughout the last two and a half years.

Special thanks to:

Jed Novick
for being able to write my story as it happened.

Pen Press
for your help with this book and enabling my voice
to get out there as I intended it.

Acknowledgements and thanks:

This is more than just an acknowledgement
but an emotional thank you to my mum, Dot and
Paul and my sister Carol, Guy, Hayley and Ryan,
Samual and Craig and to everyone who has stuck by
me, supported me and advised me over some very
tough years.

It is also in acknowledge and with thanks to all the
people that have helped in supporting and or show-
ing up at my various protests and court appearances
over the last 4 years, most notably Graham Manson
Kevin Keating
Clarrisa and Michael (from Brixton)
Andy Neil
Eddie Gorecki
Mike Sedah
Doug and Dimpnah
Pete Kelly
John Coghill
Michael Cook
Arte Miastowski
Jamie Montfort,
Joel Benjamin

and the public for voting for me in
Channel 4's 'most influential person in British politics'
2003 awards

Message from Jed Novick

Before you start reading this book or this introduction or anything, do this for a minute. Close your eyes. Imagine your children. Imagine them growing up. Imagine them getting a star at school for tidying their desk and them being thrilled about it. Imagine their friend having a birthday party and them coming home with a party bag. Imagine them losing a tooth, the bright red gappy smile and their excitement because they know that this means that the tooth fairy will come. Imagine them growing up. Now imagine all that happening somewhere else. And you're not there. You know it's all happening but you're not there. You can't see them and they can't see you. They've just fallen over and banged their head. You're not there. They're crying. You're not there. They've just come home from school and they're really upset because they've just had an argument with their best friend. You're not there. It's bath-time. You're not there. Story-time. You're not there. Bedtime. You're not there. You know it's all happening but you're not there. It's not nice, is it?

When I agreed to help Dave with this book I didn't really know what to expect. I didn't know Dave, I didn't know his situation. I'd heard about Fathers4Justice in the way that you hear about things on the news that have got nothing to do with you: it was interesting, but didn't make much of an impact on me because, well, because it wasn't happening to me. I thought these blokes who dressed up as superheroes were quite funny and quite smart and thought that, as a peaceful protest it was just about perfect: it made people notice, it made people smile and no one got hurt. I also wondered what on earth it must feel like to be deprived of your kids. As the father of two young girls, I tried to think what on earth it must be like but I couldn't really get near it. Then something else would come on the news and I'd think about that.

In the beginning of working with Dave, there was probably a small part of me that thought "Hmmm, no smoke without fire". I can't deny that. I've got friends who've split up and none of them have ended up hanging off a crane in fancy dress. They argue, they bitch, they get angry, they cry. What they don't do is dress up like Spiderman or Batman. You can't help but think something like "that's not what happens to normal people. Life doesn't work like that." And so I agreed to take on the book. If I'm completely truthful, I thought, in a detached kind of way, it would be interesting.

After all, what Dave had gone through and what he was still going through was completely alien to me. Our situations couldn't be more different. I've been happily married for over 10 years. My wife and I both work from home and we share the household and parental stuff down the middle. I've got two lovely girls who I take to school every other day and who I pick up from school every other day. I take them to their friends' houses, pick them up, moan about being nothing but a taxi driver... the whole parent thing. The very idea that I couldn't see them whenever I wanted was so alien that I couldn't even conceive of what it must be like. Every time I tried to imagine, I'd hear the kids screaming or fighting or wanting something.

So we started working on the book together, getting to know each other, checking each other out. Apart from growing to like him as a person, my respect for him has grown immeasurably. The pressures that Dave found himself under would have crushed most people. The emotional trauma, the drain would have made most people either behave irrationally or, more probably, badly. Dave has done neither. Some people might think that dressing up as Spiderman and risking his life off a crane is irrational: I don't. I think it's desperate and sad and shocking, but it's not irrational. It's what someone does when they've run out of choices, when there's nowhere else to go.

This is Dave's story. Every story in life has more than one side and, no doubt, you could tell this story more than one way. But this is Dave's story. It's his story told in his words and maybe it's true that my sympathies are with Dave. We're both men and both know what that feels like. We're both fathers and both know what that feels like. But it was more than that.

But it's more than Dave's story. It's his daughter's story because whenever adults argue, it's the kids who pick up the tab. The parents hammer away at each other, but it's the kid who gets the bruise. And that – to use one of my kid's favourite phrases – is just so badly unfair. The child gets the bruise because she's not allowed to see her dad. Her dad gets the bruise because he's not allowed to see his daughter.

Dave's story is also the story of a personal journey. I know from personal experience that having a child is like turbo-charging the journey from youth to adulthood, from kid to grown-up. When you have a child, everything changes. It's a new life – for them and for you. You become a different person. The things that used to be important aren't so important anymore. The things you used to be concerned about... None of it means anything anymore. What's important is this baby you've created. New parents – all new parents - go from being selfish to being selfless, from irresponsible to responsible. We all go through this. To have the catalyst for this change – your child – taken away so quickly... I can't even think how horrible that must be.

When I agreed to help Dave with this book I didn't really know what to expect. What I know now is this –

and it's quite simple: He's a decent, human being who just wants to be with his child. Just like me. And very probably just like you.

Jed Novick, 2006

My darling daughter,

This is the hardest thing I've ever had to write. I don't know how old you'll be when you read this, I don't know where you'll be, I don't know what you'll be wearing, I don't know who you'll be with, I don't know. I'd like to think that when the time comes I would know all the answers to those questions because you'll be with me, but really, I don't know.

That's the reason why I decided to write this book, because I want you to know the truth. I don't care if no one else ever sees this, I just want you to.

My whole life I wanted a kid. I might not have known it at the time but, looking back, that's what it was all about. Like a lot of young men, I had too much energy and too little idea of what to do with it. I ran around and got involved in a few adventures, some good, some bad, but really nothing that loads of blokes don't get involved in.

It's only when you find something that makes sense; something that you really feel for, it's only then that things start to make sense.

I poured all that energy into preparing a world for you. I helped build a house; helped build a business up... prepared a world for your arrival. I worked as hard as any man and did everything I could to make things right.

And then just as you came... you were taken away from me. I can't begin to tell you what that was like. I was sad, I was angry, I was... a million things, all useless. You were the only thing I wanted, the only thing I really needed. When that is taken away from you, emptiness is all you feel.

Believe me when I say that I didn't go up those cranes because I was bored or because there was nothing on the telly. I did it because I was desperate. Does anyone seriously think that risking your life is something you do lightly? I did it, I went up those cranes, because there was nothing else I could do. I'd tried everything else – keep reading this book and you'll see that.

I don't want to tell you what to think about me or your mother. You'll do that for yourself. I do want to tell you about the system that abused me, that stopped me seeing you, that did its best to ruin our relationship, that didn't just abuse me but hundreds – thousands – of other fathers and children.

Hopefully by the time you read this, we'll be sitting together, having a chat, having a cuddle, having a laugh – just like a normal father and daughter.

In the meantime, I want you to understand that I never gave up on you, that I never stopped loving you that I never stopped trying to be with you.

I love you. Always have, always will.

Love, Dad.

"I'm all for Spiderman. When I was in the social services for 10 years they would often give the kids to the mum and in my opinion the mother was unfit."
– Paul O'Grady (Lily Savage)

"We would not put up with it if it was Osama bin Laden. I do not see why anyone would expect we would put up with it for this man."
– Ken Livingstone

"An absolute prat."
– Richard Barnes, The deputy chairman of the Metropolitan Police Authority

"I've heard people on telly saying, 'Of course, Spiderman was a drug addict and a burglar'. What the fuck has that got to do with whether he's a good dad or not? He could be a great dad. But all he can do, pathetically in our society, to flag to his kid he's still thinking of her, is to climb a fucking bridge dressed as Spiderman. Well I think that's heroic."
– Sir Bob Geldof

"The absurdity of Spiderman is nothing compared to the obscenity of a system that deprives fathers of their children and the children of parental love."
– Melanie Phillips, The Daily Mail

"Mr Chick expresses himself in a way that indicates he identifies very strongly with (his daughter)."
– Tony Baker of Baker and Duncan,

"I believe that the father is genuinely attached to (his daughter), even though her opportunity to form an attachment to him has been limited, his commitment cannot be questioned."
– Elisabeth Major, Cafcass,

"I vote for Spiderman."
— Wendy McElroy, columnist,
Fox News, America

"With one bold and courageous act, an uneducated window cleaner achieved something no one has ever been able to accomplish – he focused the attention of a nation on the greatest social injustice in the Anglo-American world today: the way decent, loving fathers are driven out of the lives of the children who love them and need them."
— Glenn Sacks, American commentator and
nationally-syndicated radio host

"I am in a position to recommend that he should be allowed to have regular and unfettered access to his daughter."
— Dr U.A.Siddiqui, consultant psychiatrist,

"Mr Chick is brilliant with the child. He is doing incredibly well. In Woking Contact Centre he is perfectly behaved."
— Mrs Macauly of Woking Contact Centre

"He's not a bad role model. I really like him. We have fun together. We've tried to tell our mum but she just won't listen."
- Sam, nephew

"My daughter is the most precious thing in my world. I was there for the scans when she was still in the womb. I was there for her birth. I fed her, bathed her, got up in the night for her, cuddled her and comforted her when she cried. As she grows up, I want her to recognise me as her dad and be proud to be my daughter.

"Now I'm just another statistic, another dad who has no part in his daughter's life. For me, it's a living bereavement"
— David Chick

"I cannot begin to describe the awful, eviscerating pain of being handed a note…. that will allow you limited access to your children. What have you done? Why are you being punished? Why is the person who has taken the children suddenly given vast emotional, legal and financial power over the other party? Though having done no wrong, the father is semi-criminalised and punished by having his children removed from him. The children's childhood is never recoverable."

Sir Bob Geldof

INTRODUCTION

People get together. They fall in love. They build a life together. They make a family. This is what we do, what we all do. Sometimes it works and you all live happily ever after. Sometimes it doesn't. Sometimes it goes well. Sometimes it doesn't. This is the story of one time when it really didn't.

Reading this, you might think that a lot of it is the normal bitterness that couples experience when they've broken up. He said this… She said that… And maybe a lot of it is. We had major disputes about our joint material possessions – the house, a business we'd built up together. When I moved out of the family home we had the common disputes about the possessions that I'd left there. Would she pay me for them? Could I get them? Again, this isn't unusual.

What's different is Sarah. Sarah isn't a possession. Jan doesn't own her and I don't own her. Sarah is a little girl. That she's been used as a pawn in this bitterness battle, is criminal.

In some ways, I'm more angry with the system than I am with my ex partner largely, I guess, because I expected more from the system. Jan and I split up with extreme bitterness. There was no love there. Nothing. I expected her to hit out and she did. But from the system I expected, hoped for, fair play, I expected to be treated equally. I thought I had equal rights.

We'll get onto all this later, but my life before Sarah had been lacking in focus and unsteady. I was a healthy adolescent with nothing to do and too much testosterone running round. So I looked for things to do. And sometimes I found good things, and sometimes I found bad things. It's not a new story; it's just what happens. It's called growing up. I don't make any apologies and I'm not asking for anything, it's just what happened. But life is all about growing up, all about developing and learning and moving forward. I paid the price and that's how it's supposed to work.

When Sarah was born it was the final jigsaw in the story of the re-building of my life. I'd worked hard; I'd sorted myself out. I owned my own property. I had my own business. I was self-employed and self-supporting. I was, in the eyes of society, a proper normal person. I had everything I ever wanted. I was a father

I said at the beginning of this that a lot of it could be described as He said this... She said that...and that's true. But to concentrate on that side of things would be wrong. What this book is about really is a father and a daughter. By what right does a system deny a parent his child? By what right does that system deny a child their father?

It doesn't matter who I used to be. It doesn't matter what Jan and I say about each other. It doesn't matter what I think of her and what she thinks of me. Who cares about any of that apart from Jan and me? What's important is that Sarah be protected from all that bullshit. She's done nothing wrong. She's just a little girl. Why should she be punished?

What's the problem? The law, the courts, the system. The first line of the Children Act of 1989 states that 'the best interests of the child are to be considered paramount' and no one's going to argue with that. But the best interests of the child should be to see both their parents. 50/50. Why not? Who can argue with that?

The courts believe that men go to work and women stay at home and look after the kids. But it's not like that anymore.

That idea went out years ago. We don't live in a simple world where men do one thing and women do another. We all help. We all share. We all do. I was there for Sarah's scans, for her birth, for her feeds, for her baths. I got up in the night for her. I changed her. I looked after her.

The world has changed, but the law hasn't. According to recent figures, of the 15,000 cases that go to court every year, the children are allowed to live with their father in 7% of the cases.

The other thing that's got to change is that the law's got to be the law. Women – mothers – flout it all the time and no-one says anything. My ex didn't turn up for my contacts with Sarah for nearly two years and no one said anything. I was put inside for nothing real, just wild accusations that she'd made. But she was actually disobeying the law, ignoring the judge's ruling and the courts just look at her and say, "OK, carry on".

One of the reasons is that the Family Courts are held in secret. Their defenders would say that they are held "in private" with the emphasis on the second word, but in the real world what it means is that no one knows what they're doing, no one knows what they say.

This is supposed to be a democratic country, but the most important thing in the country – the family – is judged by a court that is completely undemocratic. It's a bullshit state of affairs, but you only ever find out about it if you're in it.

The other thing is because of what they call the adversarial nature of the law. It's a system that encourages people to fight each other. And because it's so loaded in favour of the mother, the father is made to feel a criminal because you want to see your child. The courts take the woman's word – always – over the man's, and if there's real bitterness between them, she knows that all she's got to do is say he's been threatening her and that's it. She doesn't need any proof, nothing.

So she makes this claim about you based on nothing and

while you're waiting for the court to hear your case… Your child has learned to walk. And you missed it.

I missed Sarah learning to walk, learning to talk. I missed all her birthdays. I don't know who her mates are, or what she does with them. I don't know anything. And why? Because I'm the father. Since she was 10 months old, I've only ever seen my daughter in a controlled environment. Is that fair for either of us?

People say that when she's older, Sarah will know the truth. Good. She will – I'll make sure she does. But we can never have her childhood again. She'll never have a fourth birthday party again. She'll never learn to swim again. I've been robbed of her childhood and her childhood has been diminished because she had no father.

For me, this story is all about injustice. The frustration I felt – and still feel – about the injustice of a system that has completely failed me and completely failed thousands of fathers like me. I didn't go up those cranes at Tower Bridge because I was bored or because there was nothing on the telly. I went up there because if I hadn't I still wouldn't be seeing my daughter. Four out of every ten fathers in my situation lose touch with their kids forever.

I wasn't going to let this happen. Not for me. My daughter was my redemption, the thing that gave my life a meaning, a purpose. But more than that, I did it for Sarah. What right has anyone got to say to a small child "You cannot see your father?" What right? At the end of the day I want a normal life. I didn't dress up like Spiderman for the fun of it.

As my brother Steven – and he's been through the same thing - said, "When you get to the court, you think there's going to be a level playing field. There isn't. Your level playing field is a sheer cliff and the blokes are at the bottom and the women are at the top."

I never trusted the system when I was growing up and that turned me into someone the system didn't trust. When I was older, the system proved that I was right not to trust it.

My ex-partner has taken away my home, my working life, my daughter, my feelings of self-respect... have I forgotten anything? And all the way through, the system has taken her side. Every step we've taken, it's been on her side. She's never needed any proof or any evidence to get the system on her side, it just was. Because she's the mother. And I'm only the father.

Earlier in 2005 when "contact" between Sarah and me had started again, my Cafcass officer said in a report "...he has indeed succeeded in his own terms". Succeeded in my own terms? My own terms involved having a child and being a father. My own terms didn't include spending over £70,000 of my own money on fighting a system designed to stop me seeing my daughter. My own terms didn't include not seeing her for nearly four-fifths of her life, for missing her first steps, missing all her birthdays, her first words, her... you name it. And my own terms really didn't include risking my life halfway up the sky.

You can call it what you like, Cafcass officer. I call it a disgrace.

PART ONE

CHAPTER ONE

Where did it all begin? This story began in 1997 when I moved into a flat in Leatherhead in Surrey. I was 30 years old and sorting myself out. After many years of running around and trying to find out who I was and what I wanted, things were finally falling into place.

Life up to this point had been not what you'd call a mess, but it didn't have much of a clue. Like a lot of blokes, I had too much energy and not enough places to put it. It's easy to look back and think about why you did this or why you did that, but at the time you just get on with it. There are a few things I've done that I shouldn't have done – that'll all come out in the story – and a few times I've made decisions that, looking back, weren't that smart. Again, that'll all come out. But before you make any judgements, before you say "He did this?" or "He did that?" ask yourself whether you've ever done or said anything you shouldn't have. And be honest. If you're going to read this book and understand anything at all, you've got to remember that that's what we're dealing with here: honesty. Being honest about who you are, who you were and who you want to be.

For me, this story is all about my daughter, a little girl who was born on December 15, 2000. I will call her Sarah in this book but that's not her real name of course. Whilst this story revolves around her, I don't want to expose her.

My little girl. Small and perfect, with curly blonde hair and a smile to die for. Whatever my life was before then, she was what made it all change. It was Sarah that filled in all the answers. I'm not a religious bloke – if you are, fine, I'm just not – but I think everyone goes through life looking for something to make it make sense. Waiting for something to happen that tells them "This is why you're here". I always had had an idea that becoming a father would do it for me. My sister's got kids, my brother too, and I always loved playing with them. We always got on great, still do, and playing with them was always just fun. Kids, they just see you for what you are, don't they? They don't look at you and think you're this or you're that because you've got your hair cut this way or your trousers shaped that way or anything. It's just natural. And when it's your own kid…

The thing with Sarah was that I made her. I did that. For the first time in my life, I made something that was beautiful and perfect. When she was born I looked at her and she was part of me, but… I made her. After all the years of being told I wasn't good enough and feeling like I'd failed and knowing that people looked at me as if I was no good and just a bloody nuisance, the teachers at school and the doctors and the system, after all that… I made Sarah.

If you're a parent you'll know what I mean. That first moment when you see your kid, it's the most beautiful thing ever. Nothing can ever come close to that. When you look at her and hold her and smell her, it's just the most beautiful thing. You look at them and you see how things are going to be. You imagine what they'll look like when they're a teenager. You think about boyfriends and all that and, if you're like me, you remember what boys are like and you'll start feeling all protective. You know that people say when you die you see your life flash before your eyes? Well, it's like that the first time you pick up your kid.

And then someone comes and tells you that you can't see her. And then someone comes and tells you that you can see her for an hour once every two weeks or something. And then someone tells you that you can have 'contact' with her.

Contact? What does that mean? Do they have any idea of what being a father is?

These state-sponsored kidnappers – judges, doctors, people who work for the State system – do they have any idea of what that means? These people tell you that you can go to a grey building that looks and feels like a prison and have some stranger bring over your child. They tell you that you can be with them for an hour or two while they watch you. They tell you that after that hour or two you must give your child back to that stranger and that stranger will then take her away. They tell you that you're supposed to be grateful for this, and that you mustn't rock the boat. That you must be good or else they'll take her away again. The two hours will become one hour. And then they write a report about you.

You sit there and you think, "What did I do to deserve this?" You think, "Why can't they just let me get on with my life? I've done some things that weren't right, things that I shouldn't have, but I did it and I paid the price. This is all I ever wanted and they won't let me near her. Will they ever let me go? Will they ever let me forget who I was and start being who I am?" You think, "I've worked so hard to change things and move forward and do all those things that people have always been telling me to do – grow up, mature, develop, put your energy into something positive. I've done all those things, so why won't they let me go?" You sit there and you think, "This isn't right."

You know something. All my life – well, the first part of my life – people were telling me that I was wrong, that my behaviour was bad, that I was bad and that I had to change. And you take it. Whatever they give you, you take it. Maybe they were right, maybe they were wrong. I don't know. But with this they were wrong. And now I was all those things they wanted me to be - grown up and mature and developed – I didn't have to take it.

CHAPTER TWO

I was born in Cuckfield Hospital on February 17th, 1967 and grew up in Burgess Hill, West Sussex. I was the youngest of three kids, Steven was two years older than me, and Carol was five years older. As a family, it was completely normal. Nothing out of the ordinary at all.

I got on with my parents fine. My dad was a milkman and I used to go out with him on the floats and that. I used to play snooker with him, football and cricket down the park. I probably did more things with my dad because, well, dads play football, mums don't, do they? But I was my mum's favourite, being the youngest sort of thing. Always got on fine with my brother and sister, no problems there at all. Every year we went to Butlins on holiday. Like I say, everything was fine, standard.

I wasn't into school at all really. I'm not stupid by a long way, but I just wasn't into learning. You have to go to school, that's one of the things you've got to do and, basically, if I'm told to do something... I make my own decisions. Always have done. I was good at maths, but all I was interested in was football.

Concentration was a problem, my mind was just else-where. I don't know if I had Attention Deficit Disorder or anything – back then people didn't talk about stuff like that. You either fitted in or you didn't – and if you didn't, you were a problem. But I didn't get into trouble there. I got caught smoking a few times and that, but never any real trouble.

I got suspended once for calling a teacher "scabby", and was caned for the same offence. I took two GCSEs – Maths and English – but I was never going to hang around. My school reports said I was a likeable person and really I was a bit of a joker at school. But as soon as I turned 16, I was gone.

I always had more girl friends than boys – I didn't really get on with boys so much. I was a good footballer though and if I hadn't started smoking when I was 10 I'd have been a lot better than I was.

My dad was a big football fan – Brighton was his team – and he took me to a few games from when I was about 10. He took me down to Brighton and sometimes to the big games up in London. Leeds were the big team when I was a kid and he took me to see them a few times and that's when I started getting really interested in it all.

I met a mate, John, down in Brighton in the arcades and he was a Leeds supporter as well and that's when I started going regularly. We used to go maybe twenty times a season in the mid-Eighties. It's funny, but I haven't been once for years now. It's totally irrelevant now. You move on. Other things become important, more important things.

I was 16 when I started going on my own, and it was a long way to go, but that was all we lived for. I did love it. It gave life a bit of a focus. I had a job at Tesco, stacking shelves. It was a rubbish job, but it was all I needed at the time. I took home about £40 and that would be plenty to get to Leeds and get back and that. I was lucky because I was never a drinker so I didn't need money for that.

There wasn't what you'd call a long-term view, nothing with a plan. At that age, blokes like me don't think so much about the future. You just live for today and tomorrow you live for today too. Leeds started to take up more and more of my time. Leeds was my team and I followed them everywhere, home and away. It became like my family, something to think about, something to talk about, somewhere to put my energy. I wasn't thinking about my future so much, but I knew where Leeds were playing.

Again, looking back now, now that I've got something proper to look after – my daughter – it seems odd that I spent so much time thinking about Leeds. But at the time it was all I had. Yeah, I had a family but this was something I could call my own. For the first time in my life I really felt part of something. I felt, you know, a sense of belonging. And it was a crack because we'd take thousands to away games and in those days it was all standing up. It was a good atmosphere, loads of jumping around and that. If we won we'd have a good time and if we lost...

I was as loyal a Leeds fan as you could get, but I was never in the Service Crew (the hard core hooligan "army"), I was never that close to that side of it, but just being there was enough. At that age, you've got all that testosterone... But I never got into any trouble. I was never convicted of anything to do with the football.

I know a lot of people look down on lads following football and, at that time, we had a bit of a reputation but it was all based on how we looked. People thought we were all aggressive and that, but it wasn't like that. I stopped going when the all-seater stadiums came in. The atmosphere went right down, and now it's different, it's all big money and celebrities. Most of my mates at that time were connected to Leeds, down where I lived, not up there. I had other mates who I went drinking with and have a puff with and that, but until around 1992 Leeds took up most of my life.

That was all a long time ago, though, and I haven't been like that for a long time. Things are very different now. Whereas before I didn't really think, I just reacted; now I'm not just thinking for me. I know anything I do wrong will affect my daughter and me.

It's funny. One of the military police rope team who saw

me up at Tower Bridge and at the London Eye, he's a Leeds fan as well and lives in Brighton. We've become good mates and go out drinking together. Odd place to meet someone, though.

My father died of cancer when I was 21. I'm not sure what sort of cancer it was, but it was quite short. How did it affect me? It's hard to say. I was running around a lot at that time, you know? My relationship with my mum was always good. My mum was the best mum you could get. She did everything that anyone could want. She's now in a nursing home and she doesn't deserve that, but you know.

When I was 20, I worked for Southern Counties Gas, and really liked that. From there I had a series of driving jobs, a bit of courier work, a bit of taxi driving. I liked the driving work, it suited me.

That's the early days, really. I got a job as a chauffeur in Park Royal, west London and that was really good. Good money, nice people and a bit of respect. I started saving, got a mortgage and bought a flat. That was it, that was me.

My life was completely ordinary, nothing different to millions of other blokes around the country. By rights, it should have stayed ordinary. I should have met a girl, settled down, had kids and that's that. My life became extraordinary but it was nothing to do with me. Well, okay, it was to do with me because I wasn't going to lie down.

*　*　*　*

I was going out with a girl called Laura Chapman at the time who I met in Brighton. She was a good girl, we got on fine, but it wasn't going to last forever. We both knew that. Maybe I should have made more of an effort with Laura. If I knew then what I know now… But you don't, do you. You just get on with it and live each day as it comes to you.

Anyway. Living below me was this other woman. I'd seen her around the place but not really thought a lot more about it. We said "hello" and stuff, but that was it. Nothing more. But when Laura and I split up, I was at a bit of a loose end and I started to see more of her. It's like that when you find yourself single again. It's not that you're looking for someone new, it's just that you're out more and you've got more time for other people. You're not caught up in your own world so much.

It was April 1999 when I got together with the woman in the flat below – Jan, her name was. Again, if I knew then... It's funny how things happen, small things that you'd think have nothing to do with you, how they can affect your whole life.

She had a dog and I'd seen her around with it. I'd played with the dog sometimes, you know, normal stuff. I've always loved animals, dogs in particular, and always play with them when I see them. One day her dad took their boxer dog, Alan, out for a walk. He'd had a bit of a drink. I don't know the whole story, but somehow he'd left the dog on a train. I don't know how he'd ended up on a train... maybe he'd taken the dog for a walk, maybe the dog liked travelling, I don't know. I doubt that the dog liked travelling as much as her dad liked drinking! Anyway, I only found out the fuller version of the story afterwards. The first I knew about any of this was when I heard her crying downstairs.

Like anyone would in the same situation, I went downstairs to console her and... I love kids and I love animals. I'd seen her around and I went to see if she was OK. She told me what had happened. I gave her a cuddle, which led to a kiss, and, you know, one thing led to another and that was that. Thanks to a lost dog and a bloke who'd had a drink, Jan and I got together.

Sitting here now, do I wish that I'd never have gone downstairs to console her? Do I wish that I had been out that afternoon? You know how many times I've been asked that? You know how many times I've asked myself? The thing is, as much as I wish I'd never have met Jan as much as I hate her for what she's done, the thing is if I hadn't have met her I wouldn't have Sarah and Sarah's the best thing that's ever happened to me.

And for those of you who like a happy ending, the dog was eventually found in Euston. Alive and well.

Those first few months were completely fine, nothing unusual at all. We were just like any other young couple and did the sort of things any other young couple would do – went to the pub, went out with friends, went to the cinema, went on holiday together. All completely normal. There was nothing about those first few months that would make anyone think that it would all go so bad. Even looking back now, I'm looking for the things that may not have meant anything at the time, but could have indicated, you know, what was to come. But I still can't see what would have caused this woman who seemed so normal to turn into this complete nightmare from hell.

Like I say, my relationship with Jan started off normal and fine. We did all the things normal couples do, the really ordinary things that mean that you're together, you know what I mean? Stuff like going to the supermarket. Boring shit, but things you do. I remember we went away quite a lot in those first few months – places like The Dominican Republic, Italy and Spain. Everything was fine, happy and nothing. All normal. It was quite casual at first, but after a few months it got more serious.

CHAPTER THREE

We'd been together for about five months when things started to go wrong. Looking back, it's not so long, is it? Five months. As honeymoon periods go, it's short. Actually to be honest with you, looking back it's a miracle it lasted five minutes. Five months? I can't imagine how I stayed together with her for five months. But you can't look back with the eyes of today. You can't do that.

It was September and I'd gone over to Holland to watch a game. Leeds was playing and at this stage I was still really into the football. So I was in Holland with some mates and having a good time and all and I decided to phone Jan. See how she was. I'd only been away a day or so, but still. You know what it's like.

So I rang Jan and she told me she was pregnant. And before the news had a chance to sink in, before I had a chance to say anything, she told me she was thinking about having an abortion. That was it. She said everything in more or less the same sentence. It was like "You having a nice time over there? Everything here's okay. It was raining yesterday and, yeah, by the way I'm pregnant but I'm going to have an abortion." It was a bit of a shock at first, but to be honest I was over the moon. I'd always wanted a family, and although it was early days for us as a couple, I didn't have any worries. I loved my brother and sisters' kids and was thrilled at the opportunity to have a child of my own. I begged her not to do anything rash, and she agreed she would think about it. But she'd already decided and that was that. Was anything to do with me? Should I be grateful that she even told me?

Sitting over there in Amsterdam, I went through a tumult of emotions - from being completely unaware that anything was happening... to being completely over the moon... to being absolutely shattered. All in more or less the same minute. Up and down. Just like that.

Another thought on the edge of my mind was that she was on the pill, so this was the last thing I'd been expecting. I know women can get pregnant when they're on the pill. I know it happens, but still it's not something you think is going to happen, is it? You think, she's on the pill, that's safe. Sorted.

If there's any one point you can look at and think, "That's where it all started to wrong" this is it. One minute she tells me she's pregnant. The next minute she tells me she's going to have an abortion. Like any bloke would, I changed my flight and went straight back home. The next day when I got back, she told me that she's lost the baby, that she's had a miscarriage.

Bang! One minute I was a man expecting his first baby, seconds later I was a man facing the termination of same baby, then finally I was a man who had already lost his first baby. What was I supposed to think? How was I supposed to feel? I'd spent the previous night and the time on the flight being really angry that she would abort my child without talking to me. Now I had to put that anger away and feel for her because she'd miscarried.

This was all extremely hard to deal with at the time, all the changing emotions and stuff, not knowing how to deal with her. This all only really makes sense now. At the time I was all over the place... I didn't know what to think.

The thing is that she knew I loved kids. We'd talked about it all, we'd talked about how I wanted to have kids, how I felt that having a kid would straighten my life out. I'd had my nephew and my niece over to stay and she knew how I felt.

This whole story tore me up inside, but when you're going through things, when you're in the middle of it all it's hard to see them for what they are. What am I talking about? In my world, you call things how they are. You talk straight. If something is black, you'd say it's black. If something is white, you'd say it's white. If you didn't like it, well... you can deal with that in different ways. Some talk about it, some fight, whatever, but you don't play stupid games with people. You don't make up stuff just to see how someone reacts.

I didn't know it back then because I didn't really know Jan and I didn't know what she was capable of. I didn't know how her mind worked. I didn't know she played by a different set of rules. She played all sorts of freaky games just to test people. I wouldn't have believed that someone could act like that, throwing freaky stuff around. You wouldn't believe someone could have the brain to think of that stuff.

The fact is, there was no miscarriage. There was no abortion. There was no pregnancy at all. Nothing. There was nothing. I had a nagging feeling then, but... I only know for 100% now, but I found out later through the expert who had access to her health records that there was no miscarriage and no abortion around this time.

Cafcass – the Children and Family Court Advisory and Support Service – have all the records of the whole family's health problems and history. I was talking to the Cafcass expert and they told me that there was no miscarriage, there was no abortion. As far as I know that leaves two options: there's either a child or there was no pregnancy. Maybe they shouldn't have told me, I don't know, but they did and that's that.

Life carried on after Amsterdam, but it wasn't the same. Something had changed. I don't know what it was and it's easy to look back and say something like the level of trust had been damaged, but it wasn't like it was – not that it ever really was 'like it was'. We split up for a little while and, life being what it is, started seeing this other girl called Kelly who lived in Shepherd's Bush.

But Jan didn't want to let go. She kept coming up to my flat but just gave me grief. I was seeing this other girl and trying to get a new life started but Jan just kept on coming. Really, I should have been harder; I should have knocked it all on the head then, but she was crying, and then she managed to get Kelly's number and started involving her. Basically that was that between Kelly and me. She said 'I don't effing need this' and so that was that. If only I'd been clearer-headed about what I wanted, about what was right for me but I guess I felt guilty because at that time I still thought she really had lost a baby. So very soon we were back where we started, and for a while it was good…

When we got back together again, there was a real sense we had that this time we're going to make it work. For my part, I wanted to make it work. I was the other side of 30 now, not a kid any more, and I'd done with the running around. I don't know what it is, but there's something inside you that tells you when you're ready to settle down.

Jan had her cleaning company and was putting her time into that. I'd stupidly lost my driving job in September of that year (1999). I was caught by the law for drink-driving and was banned for a year. Not a clever thing to do, especially when driving is your way of earning a living. It was particularly dumb because I enjoyed that job and I was good at it, but it happened and that's that.

I started a window cleaning round when the driving ban came in and this was a perfect job for me. What do you need? A ladder, a bucket and a sponge. Easy. I could work as hard as I liked – and I've never been afraid of hard work. The harder I worked, the more money I got. I was my own boss and didn't have to answer to anyone. I knew if I was doing the thing right or not, and I didn't have to have anyone telling me. Window cleaning is good on this level. If you don't do the job properly you don't get asked back. It's as simple as that. If you're prepared to work hard, you'll do all right – and I did all right.

We were getting on okay. At this time she was still on the pill. We weren't discussing kids; it wasn't something we talked about. After that last time, we just didn't talk about it. I still wanted kids, that hadn't changed, but I guess we both knew we had to see how we got on with each other.

Now the thing is with these things, if a woman doesn't want to get pregnant, she takes the pill. That's what happens. I mean, a woman's only able to conceive for a couple of days in each month. Anyway, maybe it was an accident, I don't know. There are so many things that now I just don't know. She has since been exposed as a liar on so many issues, by me, by the police, by the child authorities, by the court...

Anyway, within six months of getting back together, she got pregnant again, even though she was still on the pill. Again, I was thrilled at the prospect of becoming a father, but Jan was blowing hot and cold about it. I made it clear I really wanted her to have the child and that we would be a proper family, but she was still contemplating a termination. It's tough for a bloke to feel so powerless about the future life of his own child.

In the end, there wasn't a defining moment where she made a positive decision to keep the baby. She had dithered so much that she just reached a stage where termination wasn't an option. And thank God she did. We talked about how things were going to be and planned that we'd share the work and the parent thing together, equally. Obviously in the beginning stages she would take the greater role with the baby because that's the way it is. I can't breast-feed the baby, she can. But I was fully intending to be as hands-on as possible, to do as much as I could. I remember feeling so excited when we went for the first ultrasound scan, thinking

"That's our baby."

I arranged for both of us to sell our flats and we bought a two-bedroom house in West Horsley, Surrey. It was a lovely house, overlooking fields. West Horsley's a nice place, a safe place to bring up a child, and I really felt we were going to be happy there. We moved in together and over the next year, everything escalated. We got a new car that cost £10,000, and I continued the window cleaning as well as working with Jan on her cleaning business. It was all going really well.

The idea was that we would be a team on all levels, sharing the business and the family work. Instead of me working fulltime and Jan staying at home, we would both do our fair share. I wanted to be a hands-on father. I got on well with her family who all lived nearby. I'd go for drinks with her brother and I used to cut her mum's hedge – it was all the normal suburban family stuff. She got on well with my family, too. My brother and sister and their kids would come round to ours for barbecues. It was all very friendly and, like I say, normal.

CHAPTER FOUR

Sarah was born by caesarean section at Guildford Hospital on December 15, 2000, and I was there for the birth. I was the first one to hold Sarah. I was so thrilled. Nothing can prepare you for the feeling of becoming a father. For the first few weeks we were really happy. I couldn't believe it. It was everything I'd wanted. This beautiful little bundle that we'd made – that I'd made. She was the most beautiful thing I'd ever seen.

I don't know if you've had a baby, but if you have you can skip this next bit because you know it all already. Having a baby changes you, changes you completely. You can talk about love and stuff, you can say that you love your girlfriend or wife or whatever but until you've had a kid, mate, you don't know the meaning of the word. This little bundle, this thing that you've made, it's like your whole life suddenly makes sense. This little thing becomes everything.

I was totally happy being a dad and threw myself into it full-time. I was a totally hands-on dad and was fully involved in every aspect of Sarah's life for as long as I was allowed to be. I changed nappies, bathed her, fed her. I got up in the night when she woke up. I took her out for walks in the pram, went to the park, fed the ducks, took her to the swimming pool. All the normal things everyone does. I'm not saying at all that I was the only one doing this and that Jan didn't. What I am saying is that I was a good dad. There was nothing I did wrong. I can honestly say that. There are things in my life that I've done that were wrong, I know that. If we're all honest with ourselves, then who hasn't? But where being a dad was concerned... I wasn't wrong in any way. Just normal. Some might even say that I was more involved that many men because I was around. Because I could, and I loved it.

After Sarah was born, my life suddenly started to make sense. I started looking at things differently. Like, take the football. Years earlier, the football was really important. Leeds was really important. At the time if you had asked me why it was so important, I wouldn't have known. I'd probably have got a bit angry, like 'what's it to do with you', you know? And I'm not saying now that it didn't mean nothing, it's just that now I can see it's something you go through.

Maybe it's just because when you have a kid you haven't got time for all that other stuff, you just want to look after your family and that. Earn enough money to keep them and then spend time with them. Maybe it's because before you have a kid, it's like your mates are your family. You spend all your time with them and they're the important ones. I don't suppose it matters. I could analyse it forever. The fact is, I was just looking forward to Sarah the baby becoming Sarah the toddler, the little girl, the schoolgirl... you know, just having a daughter.

Jan and I weren't married. Did the question ever come up? Actually, it did once. After we'd got back together again, she put the question to me. The way she said it was "Do you really want to get married?" Marriage was not important to me. I'm not for it or against it. But she knew I didn't. I said, "Not particularly, no." In fact, the way that she worded it told me that she knew my answer before she asked the question.

It's nothing to do with commitment, and you can't say that the way she's been to me since Sarah was born was all down to the fact that I didn't want to get married. That's bullshit. You make your commitment by being with some-one. You make your commitment by having a baby with someone. You think a bit of paper is more important than that?

Not only was a bit of paper not important to me, but there was loads of stuff going on. What you've got to remember is that at the time we had two flats to sell, had to find and buy a house, we were putting all our time and energy into making the business work... you know, all the stuff you do when you're starting out. We were getting all the important stuff done and getting married didn't seem so important. Also, you know how much it costs to get married? We were saving money, and putting it back into growing the business, not spending it on booze for other people to drink.

Has it made any difference? To be honest with you, I don't think it's made that much difference. As a married father, you automatically have parental responsibility, but it wouldn't make any difference if we were married. The mother gets everything; the mother gets all the rights. I know from the married dads I have spoken to that ultimately it doesn't matter whether you're married or not. Maybe I'd have got a bit more respect if we had been married. People *might* have treated me like I'm just someone... instead of just being edited out of the picture, instead of being simply overlooked as utterly unimportant. Would it have made any difference if I'd have been the husband *and* the father? To be honest, I doubt it.

Looking back now, I can see I was there to keep her business going while she had the baby. I know some women do carry on working, but you can't really work straight after having a baby. Jan had Sarah and after that she couldn't really work; it was my job to keep her business going and make it successful. That's the way I see it. Of course in a normal relationship that's the bloke's job, to look after the money and stuff while the woman looks after the baby. Of course, that's the way it works in a normal relationship. But this wasn't a normal relationship. It just seemed like it. We had a nice house, we were making money, nice dog, we were having a baby and then down the line... Bang.

*   *   *   *

Looking back now I can see that, as far as Jan was concerned, if the father of her child had died around her birth, she'd have been happy. Actually, that's not really true. She wanted someone around to run the company and make sure there was money coming in, but she didn't see that as anything to do with a father, that was just a business situation. If she could have swapped the father of her child for a business partner, that would have done.

Curiously, she wouldn't have been able to wipe a business partner out of her life as easy as she could wipe me out of Sarah's life, could she? He'd have had more rights than a father over his own child. How stupid is that?!

During those early months, just after Sarah was born, there weren't any signs really that Jan was the cold monster that she ultimately became. Hormones, I suppose. And I can't imagine that anyone is going to be hard as nails just after they've given birth, not even her. She wasn't a bad mother – well, not if you don't include her trying to destroy the relationship between father and daughter. She was fine at first. She breast-fed for the first few months. She was a bit moody at times, but I put it down to her adapting to being a mum, and there was nothing particularly wrong or suspicious in her behaviour. Well, nothing apart from the throwing incident. But her general care of Sarah was fine if you exclude the throwing incident.

The throwing incident? Sarah was a couple of months old and we were just at home, doing whatever you do, you know. We were having an argument, nothing major, just bickering. Jan was sat on the bed with Sarah on her chest, and suddenly Jan had a fit or something... I don't know what you'd call it. Suddenly, she just threw Sarah up in the air from her so she landed on the bed. I was just shocked, it's not the sort of thing you see, is it, a mother throwing a little baby up in the air? I grabbed Sarah to see if she was OK and apart from the crying and stuff, she seemed to be fine.

There's that thing that parents always say, babies bounce. But it's not something you ever want to find out, is it? Not normal people anyway.

She refused to talk to me about it, and things were a bit tense. But it didn't happen again and I just thought it would all blow over. Anyway, we used to see a health visitor, like you do in the early days. They just come round and keep an eye on things, make sure that the baby is alright and stuff. Jan totally denied the incident had ever occurred.

What happened? I don't know. I asked the health visitor what they'd been talking about when she came out of the room but she wouldn't tell me. She just gave me some story about the confidentiality of the mother. I could only feel relieved that there was nothing wrong with Sarah, that nothing had happened to her.

When we were together, was Jan apologetic about throwing Sarah around? Don't be daft.

When Sarah was a couple of months old, we went to Guildford to register her birth. I'd wanted Sarah to have my surname because how fantastic would that be for a dad, to have a little girl with his name. But Jan controlled everything and demanded that Sarah would have her name and that was that. No discussion, no talk, no argument, nothing. I was gutted but what could I do? We weren't married and that was the thing. I had no rights on this one and I knew that. I guess I was paying the price for not wanting to get married.

There was one thing that annoyed me. Like all couples, we'd regularly go off and visit mates and stay with them and stuff. One weekend we drove up to see some friends of mine who lived in Barnet in north London. This was in the March when Sarah was just over three months old. We were just hanging around, chatting and hanging out. Jan says she going out to look around the shops or something and takes Sarah with her. Fair enough, but then she comes back a few hours later and Sarah's got her ears pierced. I wasn't best pleased, I can tell you. That perfect little thing that we'd made, she's barely four months old and already she's got holes poked through her? That was right out of order. It's a wrong thing to do, but to do it without telling me or talking about it with me first? I didn't understand that.

After that, things started to gradually disintegrate. It wasn't like there was this one big row and nothing was the same after that. It was a gradual change. Our relationship was never a big love story like in Hollywood; we were in a relationship with each other and through Sarah we had made a commitment, and we were just getting on with our lives. Did I ever love her? You know, I must have but right now I can't ever believe that I did. It seems just impossible that there were ever any feelings between us at all – feelings apart from hate and loathing. But we liked each other enough to make Sarah so... I don't know. And the other thing is this. Can something so beautiful, so perfect, ever come out of two people who hate each other? It's a strange question, but it's something that's often occurred to me.

Jan was acting more and more strange. She was short-tempered and sharp. She'd snap at anything and we were all feeling the pressure. I couldn't do any right. She'd start arguments for no reason, accusing me of being lazy, of not doing enough. Looking back, I think she'd decided she wanted out, and she wanted to provoke me into saying: "I've had enough, I'm off." But at the time I wasn't thinking like that. I was just worried that this would affect Sarah. Sarah wasn't a bad sleeper. It wasn't anything like that. We weren't stressed or tired or under any pressure that wasn't normal.

She was doing the computer work and I was doing all the other work, the more physical work and the business was doing well. I remember that we were also getting quotes to have our bathroom done at that time.

I got concerned that she had post-natal depression. I mentioned all this to Carol, my sister, because she was a mother and she agreed that it might be. It wasn't something I knew much about and didn't really know what it was or how to deal with it. Be nice, I guess, but apart from that? I went to our doctor on October 30 to talk to them about it, to try and get some advice. If you don't know anything about something, you try and get advice. The doctor sent a health visitor and nothing ever came of it so I figured that it was all okay. Much later, I saw a copy of his report when he wrote to the court on March 18, 2002:

"Our health visitor visited Ms Green and performed the Edinburgh Postnatal Depression scale on which Ms Green scored 7 on a scale of 0-30 where anything above 12 might indicate depression. The health visitor, Joy Edgell, of the Surrey Hampshire Borders Health Trust, wrote 'David Chick, Sarah's father, consulted with me in person expressing concerns about Miss Green on 11.10.01. I asked him how he felt Jan was managing with Sarah. He answered that Jan responded well to Sarah's needs, but perhaps she did not speak to Sarah as much as some mothers do. I had an appointment to assess Jan for post-natal depression on March 14, 2001, but due to a misunderstanding Jan was not in. I saw Jan over the following weeks at the post-natal group and felt that a further visit was unnecessary'."

So that was that then. She didn't have this post-natal depression and was quite low on the scale, so it must have been something else that was causing her to behave like she was.

In June the three of us went over to a barbecue at her uncle's house. It was a beautiful sunny day, perfect for that sort of thing. We had a really nice time – or so I thought –

but on the way back home, Jan was in a foul mood.

"That way you were flirting with my cousin's girlfriend was disgusting. Everyone noticed what you were doing."

I thought she was mad. Her cousin did have his girlfriend there, a girl called Mirella, but I didn't talk to her more than I talked to anyone else and what she was saying didn't make any sense at all.

When we got home, I rang up her uncle and said "Excuse me, did I do anything wrong at the barbecue?" and he didn't know what I was talking about. So I asked to speak to her cousin and talked to him. He didn't know what I was on about either.

The way I look at it now – that and other things she did around the time – it was all an attempt to create an atmosphere where people started to think of me as a bit of a nutter, as someone who couldn't be trusted. The other thing she was trying to do was to get me to break, to get angry with her or basically just think, "Sod it. I don't want to be around this". She just wanted me out.

Sarah was, by now, about six months old. Looking back, I think that Jan figured she could go back to work more or less full time now and so wanted me out. I'd served my purpose. I'd given her a baby, I'd taken care of her and the baby while she'd been breastfeeding and that, and I'd sorted the business out. The business was going really well now. The trading account figures for the year ending May 2001 was £36,000 net compared with £21,000 net for the previous year. That's roughly an 85% increase in income for the period of her pregnancy and just after the birth – the period I was doing most of the work. Like I said before, I'm not afraid of hard work and I wasn't just working for me now, I was working for the family. Of course I worked hard.

Still, she figured that she didn't need me any more and didn't want someone else taking a half share out of the business, so best thing is if she managed to get shot of me.

Over the next few months' things got worse and worse.

Her behaviour got worse and the attempts to get me to crack or reach some breaking point increased. Everyone's got a breaking point, a point where they say "enough's enough" or where they strike out or do whatever they do when their patience runs out and they snap. She knew that I didn't mind working hard and was ready to do that, so that was that. And she knew that I didn't mind if our relationship wasn't as good as it should have been. It didn't make me happy, but I'd get on with it. She knew that. But she knew that the one thing that I wouldn't or couldn't cope with was not seeing Sarah, so that's where she attacked me.

I'd go off to work for hours at a time, like you do, and then come back to spend some time with my little girl, but as soon as I got back home, she'd take off to the gym and take Sarah with her. She'd put Sarah in the crèche there even though I was at home and could have looked after her. Then she'd go to her mum's and stay there all day. Sometimes she'd stay there all night too, so again I didn't get to see Sarah.

How I didn't crack or reach that breaking point I don't know. I suppose even then I didn't want her to win. Like everybody I can be stubborn and when I set my mind to things I generally do it. And I'd decided I wasn't going to let this get on top of me, I wasn't going to let her beat me. The other thing is, and this shows you how long ago it is we're talking, I also thought that if the worst ever did come to the worst and we split up, then the law would protect me because I'd done nothing wrong. I wasn't the one who was behaving unreasonably; I wasn't the one who wasn't being fair. If I knew then what I know now...

Months and months of this behaviour went on - me working more and more and seeing Sarah less and less - and things get no better. Then something odd happened.

I was in Sarah's room and found this hand-written note from Jan in a really obvious place. Not hidden or anything. So I picked it up, looked at it. The note said that she wouldn't be with me for much longer, that she'd soon meet someone new and have another child. I was, as you'd imagine, upset and angry and in a bit of a panic. I was also, to be honest, absolutely stunned as to why she would leave a note like this in Sarah's room. It's not the sort of thing you'd do by accident. It was a bit freaky. Why would she write it down? It wasn't as if it was in some secret diary or anything. It was just a note, just a bit of paper.

Then I remembered something. This was one of the things she'd always say whenever we'd have a bit of a row. She'd always say something like "This is just a short-term arrangement for me" or stuff like "I'm going to be off as soon as I can anyway". But I'd always thought it was just the stuff you say in the heat of the moment; you know how sometimes in a row you say something to hurt the other person?

After I found this note, I questioned her about it, she said that she'd been talking to her mum and her mum said that if she wrote things down it would make her feel better, but that doesn't stand up. Okay, so write things down, but why write it on a little piece of paper? And why leave in Sarah's room where she knew I'd find it? No, this was again a deliberate wind up, trying to get me going.

CHAPTER FIVE

"As you are probably aware, as an unmarried father you have no legal rights in respect of Sarah" – Hedleys, Solicitors and Notaries, East Horsley, 19 Oct 2001

On October 19, 2001, I received a letter from Hedleys, a firm of solicitors in East Horsley.

"Dear Sir, We have been consulted by Ms Janette Green in respect of the breakdown of your relationship.

"Our client is concerned about your recent behaviour, which she says is moody, erratic and aggressive. Due to your past medical history of drug addiction and depression she is concerned you may be suffering from a recurrence of this.

"She believes the situation has now become intolerable. Earlier this week, when she returned from work to take Sarah to baby group she was extremely concerned that you had taken Sarah without letting her know either where you had gone or when you would return, in breach of the agreement between you.

"As you are probably aware, as an unmarried partner you have no legal rights in respect of Sarah."

That letter from Hedleys crushed me. Not because I wasn't expecting it. Not because I was desperately in love with her and the thought of splitting up was too much for my heart. No, it crushed me because of that one line: *As you are probably aware, as an unmarried partner you have no legal rights in respect of Sarah.*

Well, no, I wasn't aware, and no, I didn't even believe it

might have been possible. I had no legal rights over my daughter? Just because we didn't have a bit of paper, a marriage licence? I thought all that sort of stuff had gone out years ago. I thought all those ideas like 'living in sin' had been left behind. Obviously not.

But there were a whole load of things in that letter that were, kind of twisted, you know, and inferred. My behaviour was moody and erratic? Come on. Who wouldn't be moody and erratic in these circumstances? I wasn't being allowed to see my daughter. I was working all the hours and the hours I wasn't working, I was rowing with my partner. I'm finding strange, deliberately-planted notes in my daughter's bedroom? It's hardly the sort of circumstances where I'm going to be tap-dancing round the house, is it? Being depressed, it's just a human response, isn't it?

You want to know what the reference to my "past medical history of drug addiction and depression" means? These stories were going to come out, so let's get them out now. I've got no history of drug addiction and I've never been a drug addict. Nothing. Never. I've taken drugs, but mostly it's been what they call 'recreational' drugs, a bit of puff – cannabis. This was back when I was a kid, just out of school and a bit later, and I was drifting a bit. I've certainly never got involved in any hard drugs like heroin or crack or any of that shit. Most kids my age have smoked cannabis. A lot of them still do. It might not be legal but that's the way it is. There's no point being stupid about it or denying what's obvious. It's like I said at the beginning: before you judge what I've done, ask yourself the same question.

That said, there is a drug story and I knew I had to tell this story at some time even though I didn't really want to. But this book is about being honest, so let's be honest.

Not long after Jan and I got together we went for a weekend away in Dublin. Just a little break for a few days. Nothing out of the ordinary. When we got together Jan and I used to occasionally take drugs, it was one of the things that we did. Sometimes you go out for a drink; sometimes you stay in and have a smoke. Nothing serious or mad, and certainly nothing heavy. Just a bit of weed (cannabis) to smoke, and a little bit of cocaine now and again. You might think this is a terrible thing and maybe it is. It's against the law – I know that – and a lot of people disapprove of it. I'm not going to get involved in a whole conversation here about whether taking drugs is right or wrong, and I'm not going to start trying to justify it. Loads of people do this kind of thing, more people than anyone realises, and for a large section of the public who are, say, under 40, it's a normal regular part of life. I bet more people do it than the number of people who disapprove of it, put it that way. But like I say, I'm not saying that it's right or wrong, good or bad. I'm just saying it like it is. And yes, this was before Jan got pregnant, before there was any talk or anything about babies.

Anyway, we were going to Dublin for a few days' break. I got hold of a bit of weed to smoke and a couple of grams of coke. Just for us. Nothing for anyone else, nothing to sell or anything daft like that. Just for us. Nine times out of ten, no one would know anything about it. Ninety nine times out of 100. Well, this time was the one time. We got stopped. And searched. They found the drugs. Stupidly, I didn't hide it particularly well and put it in my wallet. Maybe I didn't hide it that carefully because I didn't consider it that important. Whatever, they found the drugs.

Like any bloke in the same situation, I wanted to protect my girlfriend and so I took the whole rap. I said they were all mine and that Jan didn't know anything about it (which, of course she did) and that was that. A bit of stupid recreational stuff and I end up with a record for drugs like I'm something out of *Trainspotting* or something. And that's it. That's the extent of my drug story. I don't know if I even need to say, but I haven't gone near drugs again. You don't need to be told twice where that sort of stuff is concerned. Like I've said before, if you do something wrong and you get caught, you pay the price and you move on. The important thing is to learn. It's like with the drink-driving thing. I don't ever do anything like that anymore. And I don't do drugs anymore. I've got something more important in my life now.

The idea though that Jan had told her solicitors that I was a drug addict... it was mad. Of course she knew I had this on my records, but she knew how it had happened, she knew the truth behind it. She knew – and I don't want to come across as noble or anything – she knew that I got it protecting her. It was a two-faced thing for her to do.

And the "past medical history of depression"? This is another story and maybe a bit more serious. Well, it's more serious to me anyway. Back in the late 1980s I used to get very down. Things weren't going well and it was all a bit of a mess. It was all, you know, out of balance. I'd be super-charged one minute, full of pent up energy and ready to take on the world. The next minute, I'd be black and down. Nothing seemed to be happening and I couldn't see what was going to make it change. This was also when I was smoking the puff. Anyway, one thing led to another and I went to my doctor and he said I was suffering from depression. In May 1992, I was caught by the cops spraying graffiti and speeding and was again diagnosed as suffering from depression. They put me on anti-depressants and I had some counselling.

In March 2002, I had a psychiatric report done – it was ordered by the courts who'd believed Jan's stories about David Chick, the mad aggressive bastard. Dr Siddiqui, the doctor who did the report, knew the whole story and wrote:

"He is basically a quiet and shy person who functions well socially and has remained free from psychiatric symptoms since 1994 and has not had any formal treatment. There was no evidence of any residual symptoms pertaining to the past.

"David is feeling stressed by his present social situation and is anxious about the outcome. In the last four year he has made a

great deal of effort in rehabilitating himself socially and enjoying stability and order in his life."

Basically, the story is this. Sometimes things happen in your life; they affect you and for whatever reason you change. But it doesn't mean that you're like that forever, it doesn't mean that you can't change back. And it doesn't mean that just because you do something wrong once, that's it forever. It doesn't mean that you're marked and that people can hold it against you for the rest of your life.

We're getting a bit ahead of ourselves, but why not? Dr Siddiqui also wrote: *"He expressed strong feelings of love and care for his daughter during interviews and stated that ever since the birth of his daughter he has played a major part in her care and upbringing. He has always taken interest previously in his brother and sister's young children in the past, and has enjoyed their absolute trust and they have not expressed any concern about his behaviour.*

"I am therefore in a position to recommend that he should be allowed to have regular and unfettered access to his daughter. On the basis of my assessment I have no reason to believe there is a likelihood of harm or neglect occurring to his daughter. He has expressed considerable affection and concern for his daughter's future well-being and is keen to provide an active and caring role in her upbringing."

Both of those stories, the drug story and depression story, were things that I went through. It's what happened. I'm not going to lie about it. But it happened, and that was that. No one died, you know? Basically… yes I had problems, but it was a long time ago and I'm all right now. Next?

The next thing in that letter from Hedleys, there was no agreement between Jan and me about taking Sarah off or whatever. That whole business is a bit rich coming from her, because she was the one who was constantly taking Sarah off without telling me, taking her to the crèche at the gym, taking her to her mother's house for the night. This whole business started with Jan taking Sarah off without telling me at every possible opportunity.

So where had I taken Sarah on this day that prompted such a bombshell letter from Hedleys? I had taken Sarah to see my mother... or rather, Sarah's grandmother. Nothing so terrible about that I would have thought. And as for her not knowing where we were, maybe I should have left her a note or something but we weren't getting on, she had never left notes... whatever. So I didn't. But whatever happened to mobile phones? We both had them and if she was so worried about the situation, why didn't she just pick it up and phone me? A normal person, if they were in that situation you'd think they'd just find out where their kid was. Isn't that what mobile phones were invented for? But – and this is strange – Jan wasn't so concerned about Sarah's well being that she bothered to find out where she was. But she was bothered enough to tell a solicitor about it months later.

Like a lot of the things going at this time, it didn't make sense. If I made a mistake it was in not seeing the bigger picture, not looking at things in the same way that she was.

Between, say, June and August 2001, there was so much going on. I don't know if she was taking advice about how to play it - I don't think she was, I'm pretty certain it was all her own doing. She's that manipulative. I don't know how far back all this was planned, but looking back there was so much that was planned or could have been planned, but I can't be certain.

There was a letter she wrote to her doctor back in August 2001, saying that it was a nightmare situation, that she was living in fear of my aggressive mood swings and all that. I'm the mad, aggressive drug-taking, depressive psycho bastard, remember?

And the reality during that time? Actually, we were having quotes to have the bathroom modernised, we'd been seeing builders with a view to having the front garden turned into a driveway and we'd been on a family holiday – the three of us – to Barrynarbor in Devon. Does that sound like a couple living in a "nightmare situation"? Where one half of the couple is "living in fear" and "terrified to return home"? She's scared to return home but the three of us trundle off on holiday together? It simply doesn't make sense!

But not much of any part of the story makes sense. According to the solicitor, the reason she decided to separate from me was because I took Sarah out for a couple of hours. So you've put up with the violence, the abuse, the drug taking, the aggression, you've put up with all that, you go on holiday with me through all that and plan to do up the house and stuff, but because I took our daughter out for a few hours without first telling you...?

CHAPTER SIX

On October 21, I moved out of the house that we'd bought together and went to stay with my mother in Burgess Hill. Without really knowing how it had happened, I was back where I'd been five years ago. Not really the ideal situation and certainly not what I'd imagined when Sarah was born. Things were going from bad to worse between us and I needed some time by myself. I wasn't getting to see Sarah, I was working all the hours – and more – trying to keep this thing together but nothing was going right. I wanted us to try and get our relationship back on track, if only for the sake of our daughter and it was obvious that the more time we spent together the worse things got. I moved out and made an appointment to go and see Relate on October 30.

I didn't realise at the time that my departure from the house represented two completely different truths. I saw it as a break, something to give us a little time and space while we sorted out this situation. I later found out that she saw it as something more permanent. I found an e-mail she wrote (on the joint company computer) to a friend of hers, saying, "Dave agreed to move out on the basis that we are having a break. I'm not sure about this though".

That it wasn't just a break was true all right. I went back to the house with my sister Carol to get some clothes and my things and found that she'd changed the locks. This was the house we'd bought and paid for together, and here I was shut out. All my things were in that house from my clothes to my private possessions to the ladders and stuff I used for the window cleaning. I knew then that this was no 'break', that our relationship was finished. I felt that I'd been basically conned out of the house. I moved out on the basis that this was a short break, something to give us both a bit of space to sort things out. But as soon as I turned my back, she changed the locks, which generally isn't something you do if you're just having a short break. From a situation where we were a team, suddenly she had everything that we had shared. It finally dawned on me that I needed to face up to what was going on and maybe even see a solicitor.

We had a couple of Relate meetings, none meant anything though. Sometimes it made it worse. On the way back from a meeting on November 14 we had a bit of a row. Having a row isn't such a strange thing, especially between a couple on their way to a Relate meeting, but she used a phrase that stuck in my head. It sat there and, for the first time made me realise, that things were going to get worse. She was saying things like I should be grateful for what little she allows me to do, that she could do me any time she wanted. I said that I was Sarah's father and that we were in this thing together. Then she said, "you'll not be allowed to see Sarah because of your history but if you want me to start playing fucked up then I really will." Basically, do as you're told or else.

We put the house on the market for £199,950 and I prepared to move on. I went back to the house to collect my things – everything was there. I'd left basically wearing the clothes I was standing in and maybe a plastic bag with a few things thrown in. Everything I owned was in that house. I went round on November 16 to see what I could get. I remember the date because she reported me to the police for violent behaviour, for being abusive and threatening and the like. I can't say that I was looking forward to seeing her nor spending any time with her. I just wanted to go round there, get my stuff and go.

There was abusive and threatening behaviour on that day in November. *Her* towards *me*. She went off the rails, shouting and making a right scene. I didn't hang around – I didn't need any of that.

That day I decided to get out and left and went to stay with a mate in north London. I'd had some bad relationships with the police around where we'd been living and I thought they'd come after me. I guess I was a bit paranoid about it all. You've got to remember, I was more than a bit shaken up by all this. My whole world had been pulled from under my feet and I didn't know where I was. I was in a panic. I hadn't done anything wrong but I didn't want to be arrested for nothing.

She reported me to the police and we ended up at Guildford County Court. This is what she said in a sworn statement:

"He returned to the property on November 16 to collect his possessions. When he was collecting these he assaulted me in that he kicked my thigh, threatened me and chased me into the garden. When I attempted to re-enter the property he slammed the door against my head. I telephoned the police on my mobile phone and he ran away. I have had to leave Sarah at my parents' home as I was frightened for her well-being with his threatening behaviour. I believe she will need to stay there until I have a court order protecting me. I am concerned that he will return to the property and I have barricaded the doors as I am frightened for my safety if he does."

As it goes, I was lucky. There'd been a neighbour hanging around, David Harris, who saw the whole thing and was prepared to stand up for me. The police report on the incident logged his evidence:

"I was unloading my car at about 2.30pm on the day in question. I heard shouting from the direction of East Lane. That is not unusual. Children are about and it was a woman's voice and maybe a murmur from a man's voice.

From the tone in the woman's voice I thought a child was being chastised or something. I saw a man standing on one side of the road and a woman standing on the other side of the road shouting. She was clearly very agitated…. I did not see the man act in an aggressive or violent way or raise his voice at all. She was behaving in an hysterical way, shouting as one would if chastising a child."

That seemed reasonable enough. I thought I was off the hook on that one – but the truth was I was just about to get my first lesson in the way that the law treats mothers and fathers.

At Guildford County Court, I was ordered not to return to the property, not to threaten violence against Janette Green and not to intimidate, harass or pester her. And just in case I was thinking about it, I was ordered not to instruct anyone else to threaten violence against her either. How did that happen? I don't know. Not only didn't I threaten her or abuse her or whatever, not only was it the other way round, but there was actually an independent witness who stood up and said so. And then I was hit by a non-molestation order!

It's around this time of the story that you'll start to think things like "He must have done something" or "There's no smoke without fire" or "I don't believe it. If the courts said that it must be true". Well, all I can say is that probably if I was reading this about someone else, I'd probably also think those things. It's natural to think that. And I hope you're never in a position where you find out the truth about the legal system and how it treats men and dads.

I realised that I needed some protection myself, and on November 20, I employed a firm of solicitors, Mahany and Co, to fight my corner. Mr MG Barrell, my solicitor, wrote a letter to Hedleys asking whether it would be possible to arrange for me to collect my possessions. He also said that I would like to resume regular contact with Sarah.

"To that end, our client would like to propose contact between himself and Sarah between 9am and 7pm every

Saturday." In order that Jan and I didn't have to meet to do this. "Our client has proposed that he should collect and deliver Sarah from your client's brother, Marvin. If this solution commends itself to your client, we propose that the first contact should take place this Saturday."

We got a letter back two days later. There was another appearance at Guildford County Court booked for November 27, a follow-up to the first appearance, and, "We have advised our client that until this has been fully heard there should be no contact between the parties and regrettably with Sarah." After that, they said, "Our client is quite prepared to allow your client contact with his daughter either at our client's mother's home or at her brother's." They soon changed their tune. Shortly after that we got another letter saying, "Neither our client's mother or father wish to have any contact with your client as they are elderly and are afraid of him and has made numerous abusive telephone calls to them." Not true. Absolutely not true. The proof? None. The evidence? None. "Our client's brother has agreed to host the contact. This is not a satisfactory long term arrangement but as our client is concerned about your client's drug-related problems she is afraid to leave Sarah in his unsupervised care."

This was outrageous. I'd never hit a woman – ever – and certainly not the mother of my child. I'm not a violent man. And the idea that I'd threaten her parents? What type of person did they take me for? All the stuff about abusive phone calls was rubbish, and I thought that that would trip her up. You can make all sorts of accusations like, "He said this" or "He hit me" or anything, and it's just her word against mine. But once you start saying something like I was making abusive phone calls, well you can check all that through the bills and stuff. I thought the solicitors would call for those and that would be that. Case dismissed. But they didn't. Lesson Two in the way that the law treats mothers and fathers.

The stuff about "drug-related problems" was a cheap shot because she knew that was something she could attack me on, and the implication that Sarah was unsafe in my care… That little girl was the most precious thing in my life and the idea that I'd hurt her…

I would imagine Hedleys and Mahany got to know each other quite well during this period. The letters started flying back and forward, all *Our Client* this and *Your Client* that. I denied the charges that I was violent and aggressive. She kept saying I was. She didn't ever have any proof. The only evidence flying between the two solicitors backed up what I was saying - but never mind about that. Nobody took that into consideration. I still couldn't get my stuff, which was a right pain even though, according to Hedleys, "The only items of your clients that remain at the property are one sweat shirt and a driving licence."

I had a little more there than that. I had everything there – including my ladders. No ladders, no work. No work, no money. Now I had no child, no house, no belongings, no income and no means of earning an income. Things were declining rapidly. Funny how when the downward spiral begins, suddenly everything seems to conspire against you. I was being denied all the joint investment that I'd made in what I thought was our joint life up to that point. I'd worked my backside off for the best part of two years on that business, building it up for what I thought was my family. Now the house had gone, the business that I'd worked up into a reasonably big – well, big for us – business had gone, my income had gone… All those things I was being denied and I was getting no comeback.

I just wanted what I was entitled to; I was just asking my possessions back that were still at the house. Things that you might think are small, but which add up to a lot. We'd bought quite a nice bed for £600. A fridge freezer, washing machine… all that. I just wanted what I was entitled to from our joint possessions. And, if I'm being completely honest, it really upset me that all that stuff, things that I'd worked really hard to earn the money to buy, she was going to get it all. A TV unit that my mother had given me was dumped in the front garden in some sort of attempt to provoke me.

I made a claim to the small claims court for £2,000 regarding all this – things that they call chattels. Shortly after I did this, Jan made a surprise counter-claim to the court for a similar amount, a claim which was totally fraudulent. She said that she was claiming against me for damage done to her car. What damage? A story. About a year previous, Jan had sacked a couple of cleaners from the cleaning business and, not to put too fine a point on it, they weren't too happy about it. A few days later we noticed that there were scratches down the side of the car, the sort of scratches you get from running a key along the side. Odds on, it was done by one of these cleaners. Either that, or some local kids. Whatever, it was reported to the police and that was that. We didn't follow it up or make an insurance claim on it because, well you don't, do you? You don't make an insurance claim because every time you do, the insurance companies kill you.

Why am I banging on about this anyway? Who cares about an old telly or a few scratches on a car? But the reason I'm talking about it is exactly that. It is pathetic. It is rubbish. We could have done anything. We could have talked about how we were going to split the house and the business like proper people, we could have talked about how we were going to look after Sarah like proper parents. We could have done anything but we didn't because Jan preferred to perjure herself, she preferred to lie to the courts rather than behave like an honest person. And that's the truth.

Something else that's the truth is that I hadn't seen Sarah for weeks.

*   *   *   *

Life at this time wasn't great. I was living with my mum and I wasn't working. I couldn't work because my window cleaning stuff was at the house and she wouldn't give the chance to get it. I'd tried to get my sister to go round there and get it, maybe you know if I wasn't involved it would be easier. Jan didn't have anything against my sister, did she? She didn't have anything against my sister but she wasn't going to help me. Every time Carol called her, Jan said it was "inconvenient". More and more, life seemed to be an endless round of meetings with the solicitors, reading letters from the solicitors, going to the court, preparing to go to the court, thinking about what happened last time I went to the court... It wasn't exactly how I thought things would be, but when you're in a situation like I was, it's easy for things to get on top of you. Seeing Sarah was all I could think about and all my energies went there.

The date at Guildford County Court came and went and nothing new was said. I was beginning to get a handle on this game. You go to court and nothing happens except you get told to go to court again. In the meantime, the solicitors get paid. So you go to court again like you've been told to and nothing happens. Except the solicitors get paid again.

Mahany wrote to Hedleys on November 29th listing a whole list of things that I still had at the house. From the ladders to the TV cabinet to my exercise stuff to... everything. "Items of personal hygiene in the bathroom" were listed. Like I say, everything.

More importantly, there was the question of contact. I'd gone round to Marvin's on the day before and it had been okay. I got on fine with Marvin and he was cool. We weren't mates really, but we got on fine. Whenever there was family stuff going on we'd have a drink and a laugh together, but still. The idea of going round to his house to see my daughter while he was watching did my head in a bit, but I was prepared to accept it if it kept the peace. I was getting to see Sarah which was more than I'd managed to do for weeks, so it was worth it. I got in touch with Marvin to talk about this and obviously he already knew. It was embarrassing –

you imagine phoning up your ex partner's brother to talk to him about seeing your kid at his house because it's been decided that you're not to be trusted. He knew all that story – but he also knew that it was a lot of old bullshit. He knew the story he'd been told and he knew the real story. But what could he do? He's not going to denounce Jan, is he? And talking to him about it… We were more used to having a few beers and a laugh, not talking about the inside of my relationship with his sister.

Mahany wrote: "Our client appreciates that he must accept your client's proposals. To that end we would invite your client's proposals for regular contact visits by return. Our client is willing to comply with any offer your client may put forward in this regard, but would suggest that twice weekly visits, perhaps once at the weekend and once in the middle of the week would be a good idea." They're so polite, these solicitors.

By return? No chance. On December 4th, Mahany wrote to Hedleys that: "Our client is dismayed not to have received a response". Dismayed? I don't think so. She was behaving exactly as I thought she would and I knew she wouldn't behave like a human being. Why should she do that? It wasn't exactly what you'd call 'in character'. Ever since this started she'd been lying and cheating. Why would she stop now?

They also asked Hedleys to confirm or deny whether Jan was planning on taking Sarah abroad. I'd got wind of this through Marvin and wanted to know. Is it unreasonable for a father to want to know where his daughter is? I didn't say they couldn't go abroad, I just wanted to know where they were going.

Hedleys replied with two pages of hostile bullshit that showed we were getting nowhere. "We draw your attention to the fact that the parties are unmarried and there is no Parental Responsibility agreement. Your client has absolutely no rights to any information… We would suggest that you point out to your client that our client can remove Sarah from this country at any time for a period of 28 days without his knowledge or consent... Our client's brother is prepared to allow one further contact visit only, to take place at his home on Sarah's birthday, December 15th, at 10am to 12 noon."

Was that true? I had absolutely no rights to any information about Sarah? Could Jan really take her any- where she wanted to for a month without even telling me? This was my daughter...

*   *   *   *

Here's another little wind up she pulled at this time. Jan got in touch with her solicitor and said that she "is concerned that I should have money to live off until such time as matters are concluded."

Concerned. How very nice of her to be concerned.

We got a letter from Hedleys on December 5th containing a cheque for £12,000, written out to me. She sent it to her solicitor. He sent it to my solicitor. Then he sent it to me. I got this cheque for twelve thousand pounds and already – well done Jan - I'm wound up by this. Twelve grand for what? The house? I'm entitled to about thirty or forty thousand. So what was it for? It was just designed to take the piss out of the system and wind me up. Should I take it, or was it part of some game? I had no choice. I had to take it.

That was when I noticed that it was dated 5/6/01 - six months and a couple of days previous. I couldn't believe it! Cheques can only be cashed up to six months after the date on the cheque. After that, they're useless. So Jan has sent me a cheque which is dated six months plus a few days... what screwy action is that? She's giving it to me because she's 'concerned' then gives me a cheque that's out of date. Some concern. Just another notch on the wind-up, hoping that it will go some way to me losing my rag, that I'll do something daft. Then she can turn round and tell everyone what an unsuitable father I am.

Not only is it a pathetic amount compared to what it should be, it's not even real. It's just another wind up. The thing was, her solicitor sent that cheque onto my solicitor to send on to me. Her solicitor didn't notice it – or they did notice it and they didn't care – my solicitor didn't notice it and it wasn't until, I told him that it was out of date that anyone knew. They're worth their weight, these solicitors. Clever people, go to college to learn and that. Know what I mean?

When that happens, what are you going to do? Phone her up and say, "Oh, excuse me. I think you made a mistake there," or what? No, no. There's no point doing anything like that. What are you going to do? Have a chat about it?

It really got to me... it pissed me off enough to do something that I later regretted. You know sometimes you do something that you know is maybe wrong, but... okay, I sent her two anonymous text messages. I got a mate to do it and one of my uncles to do it. Basically, just before I left the house I was looking on the computer – it was the business computer and I was part of the business - and I saw some emails she'd sent to her friends and she'd sent off for some information about getting her tits lifted up. So basically I thought I'd bug her just a little bit – and compared to what she's done to me this is bugger all anyway. I got, like I say, a mate and an uncle to send her text messages reading "Miss Saggy Tits" – and those were the very words she'd used in her email – and I sent her a cosmetic surgery brochure which she'd also requested herself. She wanted it, so you could say I done her a favour, sort of, anyway. And I sent her a get well card because she is unwell, still to this day. It was a wind-up and maybe it was wrong of me to do it, but compared to what she's done to me and my daughter, it's nothing... Anyway, big deal. You couldn't exactly call it abusive or threatening – or violent.

CHAPTER SEVEN

Contact on the 15th? That was nice. If she thought I was just going to forget about Sarah's birthday and sit quietly on the side, maybe sit at home watching the telly when I should have been with my little girl... I didn't want anything to do with whatever birthday plans she had in mind, but I did want to see Sarah. Can you imagine a situation where you wouldn't want to be there for your child's first birthday party? Not to celebrate that... it would have broken my heart.

It did break my heart. When you have a baby you have all sorts of ideas about the future, but I doubt very much that one of the ideas you have is that when you see your baby on their first birthday it's called 'contact'. And it isn't at your house or even at your daughter's house. It's at your ex's brother's house because the courts have decided that your daughter wouldn't be safe if she was left alone with you. It's not ideal, is it?

The official reason she gave why our 'contact' had to be at Marvin's house for this was that hers wasn't big enough for all of us and such a big number of people in such a small place would have been unsettling for Sarah. It would freak her out. What a lot of rubbish. Sarah was having her first birthday. Now, I love that little girl and all, but really, she was one year old. She can't walk, she can't talk. She's not going to be lying there thinking about the design of the flat or how spacious it is. She's not thinking about whether there's enough food and drink for everyone there, or about the decorations. She's just happy to see the people she loves – her parents, both her parents.

Really, how aware is Sarah going to be of how much space there is? Exactly. She's having her first birthday – and it's garbage. All that she's concerned is whether her dad's there, not how many square metres the flat is.

The flat's not big enough was the official reason, but I knew that what she'd told people – and what she'd led people to believe – was that if I was in hers I'd get in an uncontrollable rage and go mad. I'm saying that as if it's funny or something, but I know it's what she told her family and friends. It was all part of the plan, another little thing that made the people around her think "Hmm, maybe there is something in what she's saying. Maybe he is an out-of-control nutter". That was all part of this drip, drip, drip thing she was doing. If she says something enough times, people will eventually believe it.

I was going to say, "When was she going to realise that I wasn't interested in her, that it was Sarah I wanted to see?" but she did know that. It was precisely that knowledge that motivated her actions. And she wasn't interested in that. She didn't care. What she cared about was the longer term, trying to make sure that there's no chance that I'll get custody or anything. So that's why there's this constant talk about me being this and that, violent and drug-abusing… all insinuation and nothing with any proof or evidence. At the time of Sarah's birthday, to say I was frustrated was putting it mildly. But I paid no heed to this frustration because, at the end of the day, it meant that I could see my daughter.

So I went along with it. I went round to her brother's flat in the morning – before they were having their party – and had an hour or so playing with Sarah, just being together, me and her. I didn't want to see anyone else. I didn't want to see my ex or have to listen to any of her lies, or even look at her twisted face. All I wanted to do was see and play with my daughter. It had been a long time since I'd done that – and that was that. We hadn't seen each other for about a month at that time, and it was obvious she just wanted to see me. As soon as we were together, she just wanted to put her arms out to me, and was smiling and laughing, cuddly and happy. That's how it was. A kid of that age isn't going to sit there thinking, "Oh, the flat's not big enough."

It was a ridiculous situation. I went there and there's me and Sarah, Marvin and Margaret, Jan's mother, and a few other members of her family. It was to see Sarah, but everything else was rubbish. There was me and Sarah playing and Marvin going "Another drink, Dave?" but at the same time there were awkward silences. No one knew what to say, they were all looking at me as if I was the Devil or something. You can imagine what they'd been told by Jan, what she'd told them about what I'd done and obviously they're going to believe her. It was all going to start building and I've no doubt at all that within minutes someone would have said "I always said he wasn't good enough for you." This wasn't how I thought Sarah's first birthday would be.

Despite her mother being "elderly and afraid" of me, as Jan claimed to her solicitors, Margaret was actually okay with me. We'd always got on alright in the past and it was alright now. It was strange because of the situation, but we talked and got on okay as we always had and just had a normal sort of relationship. She wasn't hiding in the corner, terrified of this monster - but at this point she hadn't been completely poisoned against me by my ex.

The other thing is – and you've got to remember all this – is that my mother wasn't allowed to be there, my brother wasn't allowed to be there, his family, my sister, her family… None of my family was allowed to be there. Think about that. None of my family. My sister's kids, my brother's kids, no one. None of Sarah's cousins, aunts, uncles or her own grandmother from my side of the family. On Sarah's father's side of the family.

But mostly it was hard for my mother. Apart from being a parent, the greatest pleasure a person can have is being a grandparent. And my mother was being denied this basic right. Every day in every way, denied. Her grandchild's first birthday party? Sorry you can't come. Why? Because the flat isn't big enough. And no. Sarah can't go outside of where her mother's brother can see her because her father is a drug-crazed mad aggressive lunatic. Can you imagine how she felt?

The curious thing is that, at *that* time, I thought it was simply ridiculous - that I was being made a right mug of. Looking back now, I realise that this was as good as it got. Sarah had a party and I got to go. Correction... not actually to the party, mind. I got to go along a few hours earlier, before her friends came, before the other parents came, before the presents were given out, before the cake was done. Putting it like that, I don't suppose I went to the party at all. But I saw Sarah on her birthday, and not in any government centre, with supervisors, and outsiders watching the clock, ready to say, "Time's up now."

*   *   *   *

I've got a video of that time I went round to Marvin's on December 15th. As far as it went, it went fine. It was a bit of an odd situation, me going round for two hours to see my little girl at his house. But it was odd for all of us, you know, and all of us just got on with it. Me and Marvin always got on well and I was surprised when, just before I was due to go there for Sarah's birthday – sorry, contact - Mahany got a letter from Hedleys. It said that he didn't want to host the contacts in the future because "my behaviour towards him had been less that acceptable".

On the video I asked him if that was the truth.

"I've got it from the solicitors that I've offended you..." I said, letting the sentence hang in the air.

"No, no. It's not like that."

"No, no," said Margaret, Jan's mother.

"But haven't I offended you?" I said.

"No, it will be alright to do it round here," said Marvin.

"I said to Marvin that Thursday was cool," said Sharon, Marvin's girlfriend. "I don't mind but Jan said it was inconvenient for her. I don't mind at all, Dave."

Now read this next bit carefully because it's very important. If what Jan had said about Marvin had been looked into, if the authorities had even been prepared to question her word, we would never have had to go to contact centres at all. Sarah and I could have continued meeting in a normal house in a normal way. It was okay with Marvin, it was okay with his girlfriend, it was okay with his mother. Jan just made it all up, made up that whole story about him not wanting to have us there. And why? She didn't want Sarah to have a 'normal relationship' with me – and certainly didn't want me to have any sort of relationship with her.

If only I'd have had some proof that she was lying. As it stood it was just her word against mine, and as I was quickly finding out, that's not a fair fight. A mother's word against father's proof isn't a fair fight. The mother's unfounded word wins out every time.

A couple of days later, on December 17th I received a letter from Mahany talking about the whole question of contact. At this time I knew nothing really about the law and that whole attitude – though I was learning fast.

"It is the right of Sarah to have a relationship with you and to see you. The court will decide on that basis of what is best in her interest. We know that you would like to have a lot of contact with Sarah, but the court will take into account her age and her best interests." Her best interests? What could be better for her than seeing her dad? Is there anything that's more in her best interests? I can understand all sorts of things, but I can't understand a law that says it's not in the child's best interests to spend time with their parents.

I'd talked to the solicitor about parental responsibility before because basically she told her solicitor that she'd agree to contact and all that if I accepted her giving me £10,000 for everything. For the house, for what I'd put onto the business, for everything. That's what she was prepared to do. Despite the fact that I was owed at least £30 – 40,000 from the house, what is this offer other than blackmail? She was busy telling everyone who'd listen what a mad aggressive bastard I was, yet she was prepared to let me in if I'd let myself be bought off for a crap sum of money.

It was around this time that I applied for PR which means parental responsibility. What a stupid phrase. What parent doesn't have responsibility? There might be parents who have responsibility who don't behave responsibly – and I'm sure there are enough of them – but the idea that a parent has to apply for responsibility... Like everything else in this story, it's rubbish. I've been completely responsible ever since the ex became pregnant and I found out that I was going to be a father.

Parental responsibility. In the real world, it doesn't mean a lot to be honest. I thought it was important then but I've since found out that it doesn't mean anything. If you get what they call parental responsibility then you're entitled to information about where your daughter goes to school and her medical records and that. Basically you're entitled to all the information, anything you want to know about your child. You've got equal rights with the resident parent. Yeah, right. If you're the father, it's still basically a nightmare. Cast your mind back to that first solicitor's letter: "As you are probably aware, as an unmarried partner you have no legal rights in respect of Sarah." As with everything, the courts and solicitors and everyone can say what they like but if the mother decides that she's not to going to go along with it, they won't do anything. She's the mother and they never say anything about the mother's behaviour.

Did I get granted parental responsibility? Look, the most

important thing to me at the time was sorting out situation with Sarah, getting into a position where I could see her - the contact. All this was new to me. I'm just an ordinary bloke with no legal training or anything. I had no preparation for any of this and didn't really know how these things worked. There were so many things going on, I couldn't keep my eye on everything – and I had to concentrate on the important things. And the important thing was sorting out the contact. Also, there was all the other stuff in my life that was going on. Where I was living, how I was earning a living, the normal stuff. Remember, everything I had – including "the items of personal hygiene in the bathroom" – were still in the house, so I lodged that parental responsibility idea with my solicitors. And nothing happened. Like everything I asked the solicitors to sort out, it didn't happen. I couldn't go chasing them up on every thing all the time.

I put in a request to see Sarah on December 27. I knew that trying to see her on Christmas Day would be a complete waste of time, same thing with Boxing Day. There was no chance that she'd give me that. So I thought the 27th would be OK. Anyway, we were having a bit of family get together and to have Sarah there would be right because she is family. My family were desperate to see her.

Basically I was speaking to my ex's mum about all this. We were getting on and she hadn't been completely poisoned against me yet, or so I thought, and she said that she'd speak to Jan and see if she could persuade her to let me to see Sarah on the 27th. I made three calls to Margaret to have a chat with her about al this, to see whether she'd spoken to her daughter about whether I could see Sarah on the 27th. Three calls. It's not that much, not what you'd call a problem. And the reason I was phoning her mum instead of going through the solicitors was, because like I said, we were getting on just fine.

I'd not phoned her before and, after this, didn't phone her again. Yet, a couple of months later when we went to court to talk about contact and all that business, the judge turned round and said that there had been complaints that I'd been sending her "abusive calls". Abusive? On what evidence? A claim by the ex's mother? No, a claim by my ex. Had I ever been abusive to her? No. Had I ever done anything wrong to her? No. Apart from these few calls, had I ever even phoned her before? No. And yet... the judge decided to uphold the claim. He decided that, yes, I had made abusive calls to her mother. Was there any proof? No. Was there any evidence? No. Was there anything at all to back up the claim? No. So how come the judge decided that I had? He made his decision on, he said, "the basis of probability". Yes, the basis of probability. The what?

I didn't suddenly get the urge to start sending her abusive calls just because I fancied, just because there was nothing on the telly and I was bored. Maybe they thought I was giving her calls, like some Christmas present. It's just all so stupid. All I was doing was... It was all just about getting to see Sarah. And it wasn't abusive. I was trying to sort out some contact with my child, simple as that. But the judge whose findings are flawed on so many points and they just went along with the mother – like they do.

I've got records of all the calls I'd made and I'd made no calls to my ex's mum before those three. I provided those records to the court but of course these counted for nothing. The mother makes wild allegations with no proof or evidence and the judge believes her. The father denies the claims and has proof to back up what he says and the judge still doesn't believe him. There's a heavy price you pay for being a man.

It was "the basis of probability" that I'd been abusive. Oh well. The ex said they were abusive and Judge just took her side. With no proof, with no backup, with no evidence. An incompetent, biased judge makes a flawed finding on the side of the mother against the father. Nothing new there.

My lawyers? Let me tell you about my lawyers. I had to give them £10,000 – yeah, ten grand – before they took me on, as a kind of deposit. I guess they wanted to make sure I'd pay them for the work that they did and, fair enough, everyone wants to get paid for the work they do, but you don't get paid first, do you? Well, you do if you're a lawyer working for me. In case you're wondering, that £10,000 I gave the lawyers was part of a loan taken from my share in the house.

I see how it works is this. The longer they work for you, the more they earn and the more you owe them. And if they solve the case before they've earned their ten grand, well then they've got to give you back the difference. You don't have to be a rocket scientist to work out that in this situation they're going to try and make the case last as long as possible so that they get as much of that ten grand as possible. You don't have to be particularly clever to work that out. Even my lawyers could figure that one.

So they had my ten grand and basically they were quite happy. They weren't up for this. They could have exposed this story, simple. But then the case would have been over and they wouldn't have made so much money so they don't go down that route.

Did I get to see Sarah on December 27th after all that? Don't be daft. Of course I didn't. Who am I? Only her dad. Did they give a reason why not? Don't be stupid. Of course not. It was all 'we got plans' or 'we're visiting relatives'. Well, what more important relative that the father? The next time I was to see Sarah would be January 27.

It was the basis of probability that it wouldn't happen.

CHAPTER EIGHT

A new year. And it started okay. I got a letter from Mahany & Co on January 2nd 2002 saying: "Courts usually favour a party who is seen to be acting reasonably. Dishonesty and unreasonable behaviour is usually frowned upon and viewed unfavourably by the Courts". This made me feel better. We had a "Contact Hearing" at Guildford coming up on January 17th.

Contact hearing. That's a joke. A contact hearing where they decide what contact a dad should have with his kid. Who are these people who suddenly decide that they're God? By what right can they sit there and tell me that I can't see my kid? My daughter… my daughter… they're sitting there and saying, "Well, you can only see her for one hour every week," or whatever they decide. I can't tell you how it makes me feel. Basically, if you've been through it you know what I'm talking about. And if you've never been through it… Mate, do anything you can to avoid it. Anything. A couple I know who split up decided together that the woman would tell the courts that the bloke had done a runner, disappeared. That way they'd be free to make their own arrangements, figuring it didn't matter how much they rowed it would be better than some twat in a Family Court telling them what to do.

Family Court? That's also a joke. The Family Courts are all held behind closed doors. This is supposed to be a democratic country, that's what they always tell us, isn't it?

The most important decisions that are made – whether a parent can see their child, that's all done behind closed doors. They can do what they like and no one knows. They can say what they like and no one knows. These courts are held in secret. They use the words 'in private' – but it doesn't matter. It's secret.

One other thing while we're here. Contact. What sort of word is that? It makes it sound like, I don't know, something dirty. Like you've got to wear throwaway plastic gloves while you're doing it or else you might get infected. Contact. This isn't 'contact' – this is me seeing my little girl, my daughter. A parent and their child.

Still, if what Mahany said was true, it would be all in my favour, I'd been the one behaving reasonably, she'd been the one lying and evasive and obstructive. There wasn't any question about who had been the most reasonable out of the two of us. Everything – from the David Harris story to my possessions, to Marvin, to that cheque, to the nonsense about abusive calls to her mother – everything was in my favour. Bring it on.

District Judge Darbyshire at the contact hearing listened to our story, heard the evidence... and then ordered supervised contact for the first four Saturdays of the month. Two hours between 2.30 and 4.30pm, starting at Guildford Contact Centre on January 26 and at Woking Contact Centre from February 2nd. This was absolute torture. Think about it from the father's situation. He's moved out of the house. He's missing out on all the normal, day-to-day stuff, he's living on his own and all he's thinking about is seeing his little kid. Think how important those two hours of "contact" become. And think how the rest of the week shapes up. It is absolute torture.

What is 'supervised contact'? Supervised contact means that I'm not allowed to see Sarah alone. I'm not trusted to do that. I must see Sarah with a supervisor. Basically we go to a building like a church hall, in other words it is a faceless, soulless place. The very words Contact Centre make you imagine some sterile, bland horrible environment and I suppose that's the point. You sit by this table desk - and you're not alone, there are quite a few other people in the same scenario, basically other fathers seeing their children in a supervised environment. The whole thing is crap. You know you see films about people visiting in jail? It's not a lot different. You get brought your kid by some contact centre official who hands her over to you... Which means that there's another room like the one you're sitting in where your ex goes and hands your child over in exactly the same way.

It's such a false environment. It's like being in a prison visiting centre. You can't go for a walk or play in the park. You're stuck in a room with a few toys scattered around. And all around are these other men in the same desperate position, trying to bond with their children. Bond? In that environment? It chilled me to the bone. I don't know how Sarah felt about it. It's just awful.

What must a little girl make of this? I mean Sarah was just over one at this time and you might think she wouldn't think an awful lot about it, but little kids work on instinct – that's all they've got because they don't know anything else – and anyone's instinct is going to tell them that this is wrong. Obviously the kid isn't going to enjoy this whole thing. Being taken to some strange building, being taken away from the mother by some official she doesn't know. She's hardly going to see this as a trip to the seaside, is she? The result of all that is that she's going to associate seeing me with this place, she's going to think that seeing Daddy means going to this horrible place. And it's only a hop and a skip from that to "Daddy's horrible". Supervised contact? State-sponsored torture more like.

And what's it based on? This idea that can I see Sarah for two hours on a Saturday afternoon. What's it based on? It's based on the mother saying that I'm a violent, drug abusing whatever and the judge has gone along with it despite there being no evidence to support anything she's said.

It's a ridiculous restriction to place on both the father and the kid. For the father it makes the week complete torture. You build up to it and build up to it and build up to it… You can't help but be wound up and nervous and tense by the time it comes round. And for the child, what's it like? The father inevitably becomes this strange man who you see in this grim grey place while you're being watched by other people. How on earth do they expect you to build and maintain a relationship in these circumstances? Two hours a week in an artificial environment? It's ridiculous. You don't get to see them doing what they do where they do it. You get no idea of their mates or their mates' parents, you don't know anything about them. You don't know what their favourite food is. What ice cream they like from the ice cream shop. What's their favourite thing at the playground? These things that a normal parent would even have to think about, you don't know. Who are you going to ask? Your ex? Don't be stupid. She wouldn't tell you. She's the one trying to destroy your relationship, not truing to help it. Are you going to ask that guard, sorry the contact centre helper? What do they know? You're just a number to them, one of many that are supposed to turn up on a Saturday afternoon between 2.30pm and 4.30pm. Basically, this contact at a contact centre story is something that the State throws you but in reality it's more of a tease than anything else. Here's your kid. Look at her now… And now she's gone.

I just said "How on earth do they expect you to build and maintain a relationship in these circumstances?" and the answer is "They don't."

I've got to say this. If I'm all the things that Jan has claimed I am, I'm amazed she's happy for me to see Sarah at all? If that was me, if the role were reversed, if I was the perfect mother and she was this violent, aggressive, drug abusing whatever… I wouldn't let her come in the same town as my kid. Why on earth would I let my kid see someone like that? It's just more contradictory rubbish. That's all it's ever been.

Still – and given what I've just said this will sound a bit rich – I was up for it. Two hours a week with my girl? Are you having a laugh? Of course I'm going to go for it.

Amazingly, even this little crumb of bollocks wasn't something Jan wanted. She really did want to wipe me and Sarah out of each other's lives. Mahanys confirmed that "Ms Green was not prepared to agree to contact, but was persuaded to do so. This is good news." Good news for him maybe. I knew that if Ms Green had been persuaded to do something she didn't want to do, she'd up the pressure on me. She'd try even harder to make them think I was a bad man, not a person who should be allowed in the same country as his kid.

"Ms Green" made allegations of harassment – legal for saying that I'd been threatening her. Apparently she also said that I'd been sending her "unpleasant" things in the post. There was only one unpleasant thing round here: her lies. Of course I didn't do any of these things, but she'd sussed by this stage that she could say anything and no one would ever ask for proof or evidence. She also knew that if she kept saying these things, people would start to believe her. Drip, drip, drip.

*   *   *   *

January 26, 2001. That was the date of the first supervised contact. I didn't sleep the night before. Well, you wouldn't, would you? It's not like I was nervous or anything. I hadn't seen Sarah since last year. I had an hour with her on her birthday and since then... nothing. That's six weeks ago. What do you wear? What do you take? Do you give her anything? Any presents? What are you going to talk about? This was ridiculous. Sarah was just over one year old. I was supposed to sit here in this contact centre and talk to her for two hours? The joy of being with a child that age is playing with them, taking them places and watching their faces light up. You don't have to talk, you just have to be. How on earth were we 'just going to be' in this place?

I got to the centre early, obviously, and prowled around outside, smoking and nervous and feeling just about every emotion there is. I went into the centre and was shown where to go. I sat down where they told me to sit down, and waited.

This is the contact I've been fighting for and it's so… lacking in humanity? That's an understatement. If there are problems between parents and contact centres are needed, then all well and good. If someone could be at risk with their child, then OK. But that's never been the case with me. And there's never been anything – apart from my ex's lies – that's said there was.

"What name?"

"David Chick."

"OK, go over there and wait."

That's it. That's what they say and, yeah, you go and over there or whatever. And you sit down and you wait for Sarah to come in. It's really cold, totally lacking in any understanding of the situation. There are other fathers there in the same situation and the atmosphere is incredibly tight and tense. All these dads, waiting. Probably none of us had slept; probably they were all like me, just waiting. I got inside this place and looked around. It seemed ridiculous to that that I was even here. What was I doing here? Again and again, the questions go round your head - how did this happen? – but all the time you're thinking "I'm going to see Sarah soon."

At this stage I didn't know what the story was, what the procedure was, so I was sitting there expecting the see Jan or her mum to come in holding Sarah. So I was looking round, bracing myself and trying to control myself so that I wouldn't say anything to Jan when she came in. After a few minutes I saw this contact centre helper standing next too me holding this little girl. I remember glancing at them before turning back to look at the doorway, waiting for Jan and Sarah. I looked at the little girl again and thought, "Oh, she's got her ears pierced just like Sarah." I was thinking it was just another little girl here to see some other poor bastard father. Then I realised it was Sarah. This little girl who'd been next to me for about 20 seconds while I was waiting for Sarah actually was my daughter. This was one of the most freaky, disturbing things I've ever felt.

I don't want to over play it, and it was only about 20 seconds or so, but it completely freaked me. There were obvious reasons why I didn't recognise her. Like I say, I hadn't seen her for six weeks, and during that period she'd just started to walk and when that happens a kid loses a lot of that early puppy fat chubbiness that they've got when they're born. (Incidentally – did you catch that? How we just glossed over the fact that I missed Sarah learning how to walk and taking her first steps. Just another thing I missed out on). Also, her hair was different from the last time I'd seen her. Those two things, combined with me not expecting to see her come in the way she did and the strange environment, the strange feelings I had being there, the strangeness of the whole situation. I'm not trying to make excuses, just... you know. It was all strange.

But however bad I felt for myself, I felt worse for her. What must it have been like for that little kid? God knows what it must have been like for Sarah. She was obviously in a strange environment, probably scared. She hadn't seen her daddy for six weeks and here he was, seemingly not interested in her.

For me at the contact centre, it was all about mixed emotions. There I was, seeing my little girl for the first time in six weeks – and I can't even begin to tell you what that was like – but... two hours in this awful environment with these supervisors? I wanted to be down the park, playing with my girl, holding her, like a normal person, like a proper dad. Taking her to see my family... At the same time, it was lovely seeing her. It was the strangest experience I'd ever had, but still, it was lovely seeing her. Holding her. Just being with her. As I left, I thought to myself, "Well, I'll get used to that. If that's what it's got to be, then that's what it's got to be." How incredible that I was prepared to accept this dreadful set up. It was rubbish in so many ways, but if it was the only thing I had, I'd deal with it.

Obviously, Jan thought the same thing. Obviously she thought that I'd deal with it, that I'd get used to it and use it to build a relationship with Sarah. I know this because she didn't turn up the following week. Or the week after that. I know, because I was there. Week after week.

The next contact was due the following Saturday – February 2 – and, again, I got there early. I went inside the building, had a look around to get a bit of a feel for the place and then went outside to have a smoke. I was standing outside the building, having a fag and a chat with one of the centre helpers when I saw her car pull up. She turned into the building car park, saw me and in the same move… drove off. Who did she expect to see? Father Christmas? Of course she's going to see me. That's what she's there for. It's not going to be a complete surprise that I'm there. Minutes later, she phones up the contact centre and says she's not coming in because I've just threatened her.

Later, she changed this to "an insult" but neither had occurred because actually what had happened was nothing. She's made a lot of false claims but surely no-one could believe that I could have a fag and a chat with a bloke whilst at the same time threatening and insulting someone else – without anyone seeing? Surely nobody could believe her claim this time? Even my solicitor contacted the centre and they confirmed that my story was true, that I was telling the truth. They asked the helper I was with and he confirmed it in a written, signed statement.

The centre helper's name was Stuart Alexander and his statement read:

"I remember Mr Chick turning up for contact about half

an hour early. I checked him in and told him to wait with the other visitors. In the intervening period before his contact was due to start, he came over and we had a chat before he went back to his seat. He then returned the door and said he was going outside for a cigarette. By this time all the people who were going to have contact visits had arrived and there were no newcomers. I remained standing at the door and could see Mr Chick outside. I remember saying to him before he went out to be careful in case the other party arrived as he would not want to come into contact with her. I remember that Mr Chick then rushed back saying that she had arrived. She was late for the visit as all the other visits were currently taking place. He went back in to resume his seat and subsequently it transpired that the other party had left the building without contact taking place."

On February 7th we received a letter from Hedleys. "Whilst our client intends no disrespect to the court, due to being threatened by your client when she attended the last contact centre visit, it appears unlikely that our client will attend this week." No disrespect to the court? That's funny. It amazes me that solicitors like Hedleys can do this sort of stuff, say these things that are just lies and get away with it. Couch it in adequate terms of respect and abeyance and everyone simply accepts it. Is there no law against them? And what do they care? It's not their life and, on the "basis of probability" they were probably just trousering the cash the same as the other solicitors were.

Talking of the other solicitors, what did my solicitor do? Nothing. He did nothing. In fairness, he did say that this was what my ex could do and he did write a letter to Hedleys saying, "It is our clients case that your client has no real intention of complying with her duty to promote contact in the child's best interest and that is wont to fabricate allegations in order to excuse her breach of the order." Another letter that counted for nothing but it was another letter sent and that had to be good for a few more zeroes on the bill.

CHAPTER NINE

All the time Jan kept inventing stories trying to convince people that I was an unsuitable father, and that I shouldn't be allowed near Sarah. She invented a story that I was threatening to kill her. Really! Maybe I should have been glad to see that I wasn't just bothering her with petty threats and dodgy phone calls, that now I was threatening to murder her. I guess there no point messing about with these things, is there?

She said I was outside her house at 9.30pm one night in January, and she was terrified. Not so terrified that she called the police or anything. Now you would call the police, wouldn't you if there's someone outside your house threatening to kill you. You'd have thought so. If it actually occurred. And did it occur? No. Was I there? No. And if it didn't occur, that explains why she didn't call the police. Simple as that.

It just shows how stupid she is because if you're going to make an accusation like that you'd call the police and then when they came, you'd say something like, "Well, he was here but he's gone now." That's the thing. It's not even clever. That's the thing that gets me about this whole story. She's doing all this in the laziest of ways; she's not even being clever yet still she gets away with it, and still the system supports her unquestionably.

Why do these stories of hers make a difference when all the proof I've got – like that written statement by Stuart

Alexander – count for nothing at all? Why did a story like that not even make people wonder about her other stories? Because I was no-one. Nobody. An unimportant man. I didn't count. Because, as I was coming to realise more and more, the system supports the mother at the expense of the father. It's like in the normal law when you're supposed to guilty until proven innocent. Well, in the family courts, the mother is innocent even if proven guilty. And the dad is guilty. Always. Simple as that. Everything else – all the court hearings, all the contact hearings, all the letters flying about – these are all just things that go on just to make the people working in the system rich. It seemed the only possible explanation for everything that was going on.

There was a story about abusive calls. Basically my ex logged eight calls and she said they were from my landline. It's not true. I got the itemised bills for this period that showed not one of these calls had occurred. Then she came up with another story. She made out she'd been getting abusive phone calls from blokes – calls basically saying that she was a prostitute and offering her services - and said that I was behind it. She said that her number had been written in some toilet and she was getting all these calls. The police went down to this toilet within an hour of the allegation being made and there's no sign of it ever being there. The police report said: "There is no evidence to prove Mr Chick's involvement." So what that was all about, I've never worked it out to this day.

What's it for? Has she started to believe the story herself? I wouldn't like to try and get inside her head. It's not a place I'd want to go to, know what I mean? But it's another one of those things that adds another thin layer to the 'I'm scared of Dave, he's a maniac' story. It doesn't need to be true, doesn't need any back up or evidence but it's just a story that adds another layer. The drip, drip, drip effect. If she says Dave's a threatening bastard enough times, it gathers its own momentum, and people start to believe it.

This is all nonsense, just bullshit. It's all designed to detract from the central story which is that I want to see my child. And all this is just one person's big fucked-up game. It's a game and a story and nothing else. It's all a game which is supposed to make everyone take their eyes off the ball and the ball is Sarah. That's what you've got to remember.

Why would I threaten Jan or abuse her or do anything like that when I knew that anything I did might threaten my chances of seeing Sarah? Why would I let anything get in the way of that? If there was even the possibility of something threatening me seeing Sarah... Come on, there's no way I would have done it. Why would I make a threatening phone call? These things are so easy to track. Why would I do that? Yes, I hated Jan for trying to destroy my relationship with Sarah and for trying to destroy her daughter's relationship with her father. But at the end of the day I didn't care about her. I cared about Sarah. If it wasn't for Sarah I'd have nothing to do with that woman. Anything I did or thought, it was all about Sarah. It wasn't about Jan. She wasn't in my life.

Think about it. Why would I do anything that threatened me seeing Sarah? Either I didn't really care about seeing Sarah or I was some out-of-control schizo who had no control over my actions. And if I was that out-of-control schizo doing these mad things, wouldn't Jan have some proof of it? Actually forget all that. Whatever the reason, if any of the things Jan accused me of had actually happened she'd have had the proof. Doesn't matter why I did it, she'd have the proof. But she didn't have any proof because none of these things happened. But more and more it seemed not to matter whether she had any proof. More and more it seemed that the system would believe her regardless. The courts have never had their eye on the ball, because they're so concerned with going along with her and her flawed bullshit all the way through, despite the lack of any evidence anywhere.

*   *   *   *

There was an odd thing about that first contact I had with Sarah. Not only did Jan come but all her family came too. They came to watch me be with Sarah. This was odd because she's with them all the time, they can see her anytime they want. Were they there just to remind me that my family couldn't ever see her? Just to upset me? Mahany wrote and warned me not to react as "this was clearly intended to antagonise you".

I made an application – not for the first time – for some of my family to be allowed to see Sarah. My mother, Sarah's uncles and aunties, the whole extending family who should be bonding with Sarah and who Sarah should be bonding with. All these people were being denied as well – and Sarah was being denied them.

Jan, my ex, said, "No."

Hedleys: "….She is not happy at the prospect of your client be accompanied by any of his family due to the intimidation she has been subjected to in the past."

The intimidation she has been subjected to in the past? Sorry, did I miss something? Did something happen that no one told me about? That time when my mother went round her house with a baseball bat and had her up against a wall, where was I when that happened?

Intimidation? From my mother? My brother? My sister? Their kids maybe? Did she say this with a straight face?

My mother is an elderly lady who is, without going into it all, a bit fragile now. Old people like that, you know, they don't have a lot to live for, and seeing their grandchildren is maybe the biggest thing that keeps them going. When was the last time she saw her granddaughter? It was so cruel to deny her, so cruel to deny Sarah too. My mum won't be around forever and these years are the time when they're supposed to be getting to know each other. Tell me this. What happens if by the time they change the law and correct these injustices, my mother's gone? Sarah will have been denied her grandmother forever – and no one can give her that back. No one can offer any compensation for that. It makes me so angry writing about all this, not only the way that my ex has behaved – she's not a nice person, and that's to put it mildly – but he way that the courts and the system has backed her up. How can the system say that it's OK to deny a grandmother her grandchild? This is supposed to be a civilised, caring society?

It was so upsetting. Not just to me, but to everyone. So I made another application. This time Jan asks who I'd like to attend. I don't know whether she took advice, or maybe she just thought that this wouldn't look too good in front of the courts. Whatever, so she asks who I'd like to attend the contact meetings. (Not that there have been any contact meetings because the ex won't turn up to them, but anyway).

I made a list of who I'd like to come and a week or so later I got a letter from my solicitor that states that Jan won't agree to "any of Sarah's family on her father's side" attending. So first she ignored all my requests to have my family see Sarah. Then she asked who I'd like to come. Then she says that none of them can come. If none of them can come, why bother asking who I want there? It's all just a wind up.

But no one ever says anything. The family courts don't do anything. The contact hearings don't say anything. Nothing. She is denying Sarah her granny. And denying her granny Sarah. You know what it's like when grandparents get together with grandchildren. And imagine being that grandparent who's being denied?

The fourth week of supposed 'contact' although by this stage I'd had one. It was February 16. I was driving round the M25 on my way to the contact centre when my mobile phone went. It was the contact centre saying that they'd just received a call from my ex saying she wasn't going to the contact because she doesn't know where it is. Am I supposed to laugh at this? She phones up the contact centre where the contact is due to take place to say that she doesn't know where the contact is due to take place. Funny that. Funny how she can find them well enough to phone them. Funny how hundreds of people find it every week. Funny how I always knew where the contact was due to take place. So bloody funny. Not.

After looking forward to seeing Sarah all week, this is absolutely gutting, so utterly gutting. To want... to want... to want... to build up and build up and build up... and then for it not to happen... This is an absolute joke.

Can you imagine what a court of law would say if it was me behaving like this?

Now there were two contact centres, one in Guildford and one in Woking. So instead of her phoning to say she wasn't coming in, why didn't she just say, "Is contact at your centre or the other one?" it takes the same amount of words, the same amount of breath. And why didn't the contact centre say, "It's here. We're waiting for you." Or alternatively, "It's at the other centre." Why didn't they say that? It's like no one cares, no one cares except me because it's me who's the only one losing out. Well, me and Sarah – and Sarah is just over a year old so she isn't going to phone up and complain. They're all abusing Sarah and me, and no one does anything about it. Another contact lost. It was all bullshit. Who was acting on Sarah's behalf? Who was looking after her best interests?

It went downhill even further and faster after this.

As my solicitor Mark Barrell wrote that February: "I remain of the view that Ms Green has full intention of obstructing and interrupting contact on any excuse." You don't say. Good spot on their part. They earned their money that week.

*   *   *   *

In March 2002, we had what's called "Contact Finding Of Fact" hearing at Reading. You might think that that sounds promising. You might think that Contact Finding Of Fact means they'll find out the facts of the contact. How it was going, stuff like that. But no. The purpose of this exercise was to find out whether all or any of the allegations the ex had made about me with regard to drugs or violence were true. Basically, Jan had been pulling all these strokes, accusing me of this and that, not showing up for contacts that had been ordered, stopping my family seeing Sarah... and no one says anything. But because of all the allegations she's made about me, we're having a special hearing.

Just before this, on March 5, I'd had a psychiatric report done. Mahanys had sorted this out for me because Hedleys had been pushing for this for ages. It was, I guess, supposed to be the proof that they wanted to show that I really was a mad aggressive bastard.

Dr Siddiqui, the doctor who did the report, wrote:

"He is basically a quiet and shy person who functions well socially and has remained free from psychiatric symptoms since 1994 and has not had any formal treatment. There was no evidence of any residual symptoms pertaining to the past.

"David is feeling stressed by his present social situation and is anxious about the outcome. In the last four year he has made a great deal of effort in rehabilitating himself socially and enjoying stability and order in his life."

"He expressed strong feelings of love and care for his daughter during interviews and stated that ever since the birth of his daughter he has played a major part in her care and upbringing. He has always taken interest previously in his brother and sister's young children in the past, and has enjoyed their absolute trust and they have not expressed any concern about his behaviour.

"I am therefore in a position to recommend that he should be allowed to have regular and unfettered access to his daughter. On the basis of my assessment I have no reason to believe there is a likelihood of harm or neglect occurring to his daughter. He has expressed considerable affection and concern for his daughter's future well-being and is keen to provide an active and caring role in her upbringing."

Dr Siddiqui's report cost me £500 and it was £500 I could barely afford, but it had to be done. Also, the fact that he wrote positive things about me did soften the blow. If I'd have spent £500 and he'd have been negative about me, that would have been one thing, but "I am therefore in a position to recommend that he should be allowed to have regular and unfettered access to his daughter"? That was good to hear.

Mahanys sorted me out a barrister, Dafydd Griffiths, and in a report he made on his closing statement he said: "I invited the HHJ (Judge Critchlow) to find that there was no independent evidence in support of the Respondent's (Jan) allegations of violence, there was no medical evidence in support and no domestic violence convictions recorded against the Applicant (me). I made submissions that there had been no drug usage by the Applicant since the child was born and that the Respondent had failed to prove her case in relation to the alleged abusive calls etc. I made submissions that the Applicant's evidence was consistent and truthful and that his blanket denial of any violence by him should be favoured. Furthermore, I invited the HHJ to find that there was no evidence in support of the fact that the calls made to the family (withheld number from a different number were made by the Applicant."

The HHJ – Judge Critchlow – found: "Having made such findings I am clear that from what the Respondent says that should she be satisfied that then Applicant is not taking drugs and that there is a safe place for contact outside the centre then she has no objection to contact. The Applicant has the child's best interests at heart. The relationship depends on him."

So… it's up to her. What that all meant was this. The judge ruled that if Jan was happy that I wasn't taking drugs and that I was not violent then she'd let us have normal contact. And if she wasn't, she didn't have to. She was the one who'd let us have contact? Wasn't that his job? Anyway, she was likely to say "Dave's being really good now, let's have loads more contact" wasn't she?

More, I was found guilty of violence for that occasion back in November 2001 when I was in the house and she was trying to attack me. I was in the house, she was attacking me and the judge found me guilty. Why? Because of the 'balance of probability'. That's the term they use. There was no proof. No evidence. No marks on her ever to this day. No marks, no cuts, no grazes have ever been witnessed by any doctor, health visitor, police… no one. The police report from the time showed that they turned up and they didn't find anything. There are absolutely no indications that I actually was violent, but the judge said that the 'balance of probability' was that I was guilty. And this is the country where you're supposed to be innocent until proven guilty. There was no finding about drugs.

So that was that. I'm guilty of violent behaviour – but only probably. That was all the Finding was supposed to be about, but somehow there were another couple of things talked about that wasn't even supposed to be talked about. The story about the eight logged calls she said were from my landline and the story about the writing on the toilet wall, these were both heard and the judgement went against me. Why? The balance of probability. Of course.

So he's talking about a 'balance of probability' but virtually everything he's found against me is flawed. You got the police saying there's no involvement by me, there's no evidence of half of it, these calls, there's no evidence of any of it, the violence is her against me, it's all clear to see, yet he's found against me. And what's my crime? Well, other than being a man, other than being a father, I don't know.

What really gets to me is that not only was there no proof, but the police actually stated that it was nothing to do with me, that I had no involvement, and still this arsehole judge finds against me. This is again on that "balance of probability" thing. She's the proven liar. Why is there no "balance of probability" about her doing the same thing again?

The balance of probability was always against me. Fathers find that out pretty quick. If a woman's pissed off at her ex or if she wants to get him banged up, all she's got to do is shout "he threatened me" or "he abused me" or – if she's really nasty – she'll make reference to "sexual abuse". Yes, and Jan did this too. She needs no proof, no evidence, nothing. It's enough to say it and I know loads of blokes who've been banged up because of this.

At this hearing I had a kind different experience. Jan had made claims that I'd been making threatening and abusive calls to her. And the Good Judge found me guilty. Again, the balance of probability. It didn't matter that I had the itemised bill from my landline where Jan claimed the calls were from to show that I hadn't called her at all. I was still found guilty.

What happened to Dr Siddiqui's report? Nothing. It was deemed "inadmissible evidence" because her solicitors didn't okay it all first. Inadmissible. That was £500 down the drain. That was a positive character reference ignored. That was bollocks. Shouldn't Mahany have known about this? Weren't they solicitors?

The joint effect of these last two things was that I was seen firmly as the bad man. Character reference? It counted for nothing because of my solicitor's incompetence. It counted for nothing because of the bias of the system and a biased judge. Verdict: Guilty of being a man.

The judge did get one thing right when he stated "The impression I form [from Mr Chick] is that he is concerned to have contact with his child."

CHAPTER TEN

She must have come out Reading Court thinking, "This is so easy." Basically, she'd been given the green light by the courts to do as she pleased. The contact that had been ordered by the courts, that was "in the child's best interests", she'd laughed at that and the courts had done nothing. The lies she'd made up about me, they'd agreed with her. I didn't really see this as a good day out, but Mahany described the outcome of the Hearing as "by no means disastrous" because the Contact Order wasn't messed with. The Contact Order that she ignores, that no one enforces. They said that because the Judge did not disturb the existing contact order, this was "effectively a result in your favour". Forgive me, but I couldn't quite see it like that.

It makes you think that the judges make their mind up before the case is heard, before any of the evidence is read out and decide that they're going to be on the mother's side, regardless of anything that's been happening. It's just an unwritten rule. Without all this bullshit, if you've got a mother and a father going to court fighting for their child, it's a nightmare for the father. And with all this bullshit...

You'd think that for a father to be in the position I was in at this time and get any sort of result, he'd have to be like the Archangel Gabriel but it doesn't really matter. Without going into his story – because that's up to him to tell if he wants to tell it – but my brother's squeaky clean; he's never been in any trouble with the police or anything and he's had a nightmare with his three boys and his ex as well. For a bloke to stand a chance in that position, you've got to be... a woman, basically. It will get changed; little by little it will get changed. It's too late in my case but I've done what I've done also to help tomorrow's fathers and kids so they don't have to go through this bullshit.

The barrister who attended this hearing, Dafydds Griffiths, charged me £1400. She said in court that she'd done everything to encourage contact and he's backed her up. How? Why? Huh, why do you think? Do you think the easier option and quick buck for a morning's work had anything to do with it?

In Mahanys' letter, that one where they said it was a result in my favour, they said they were worried – and that's in quotes – that I'd dwell on what had happened rather than, as they said, concentrating on improving the situation and addressing the concerns raised. And what were the concerns raised? The concerns were that I was violent – which I was shown *not* to be – and that I've got a problem with making abusive telephone calls – again, there was no proof that it was anything to do with me. How can I address these concerns? How can I make right a situation that doesn't exist in the first place? Have they all forgotten that all I want to do is see my daughter? Mahany also said, "It is wise to avoid getting too bogged down in recriminations arising out of bitterness." It might be wise but it's hard. She kept getting away with it and I kept getting shafted.

If you're thinking, "How can a barrister say something so contradictory to the evidence? It doesn't add up," you're right. I'd probably be thinking that too. But the point is that this is all in private. There's no one checking on them. You don't know. The only people who know are the people who are there. The secrecy is what's causing it. There's no accountability. They can do what they want. And everything is so loaded in favour of the mother that it really doesn't matter. I'm the father with no rights. Remember what her solicitor said at the beginning - as you are probably aware, as an unmarried partner you have no legal rights. I've done nothing wrong, I'm doing everything I possibly can to get my paltry two hours a fortnight with my daughter and they're doing all they can to stop me.

The barrister didn't tell me that there was an appeal procedure regarding all this. When I eventually found out it was too late. Basically you get about four weeks or something to organise an appeal against the decision. I was trying to sort out my contact, I was trying to sort out my house, my possessions, some work, all this sort of stuff and, you know, I don't know about the law. I don't know about appeals procedures. That's why I employed these solicitors and barristers – they're supposed to be the experts. That's why I signed over £10,000. And that's why I sacked all these people shortly after this.

On April 17th I decided to sack Mahany and represent myself. Was this a good idea? I don't know. They've been to college, they've studied the law, they've got the letters after their names. What have I got? Nothing compared to that, but what I have got is an interest. I care about the case and what's going to happen; I don't just care about the pay cheque. I'd gone for solicitors and barristers and all the people you're supposed to trust and they'd done fuck all, got me nowhere. So now I'd try and do it all myself and see what happened with that.

At this time I was working as well – for Gregg's bakery up in Twickenham, delivering cakes and bread – so it was a lot to take on. But it doesn't matter whether you represent yourself or you've got solicitors, in the family court you lose. If you're a male, you lose. The only thing I didn't find out was whether I had to pay myself ten grand for doing fuck all.

I didn't have any advice or any back-up. No. I just knew I couldn't have them represent me no more. I'd paid out over £6000 to Mahany and Griffiths and it had got me nowhere. I just thought I know my case better than anyone, and I know that I care about my case better than anyone so why not? It was a bit of a worry that I didn't know the legal language but then I looked at it that I'd had these experts, these people who'd been to university to learn that language, and they'd done jack shit, and you know, it doesn't matter whether you've professional solicitors or you represent yourself, a male in the family court, they just shaft you. Every time, simple as that.

On April 20th there was a contact at Woking Centre. I'd been representing myself three days and already something good had happened. Sarah came into the centre and I looked at her and she had a two inch graze running down the middle of her face. Obviously, I was alarmed. Well, you would be. I hadn't seen her for how many weeks and then when I do she's got a two inch cut down her face? Course I was concerned.

I got in touch with Mrs Quinn, our Cafcass officer, and expressed my concerns. Apparently, Jan had told them that it happened when Sarah fell against a slide. A slide? I didn't believe that. Slides in children's playgrounds have all rounded edges, you don't get scratches like that from a small kids slide. Maybe if she was on the big kids slide? Maybe you can bump your head or something if you fall, but not scratches like this. I know how the cut happened. Their dog did it. Now I love the dog – the dog's never done anything to me – but it was obvious that the dog had done it. The dog sits there and puts its paw up when you're playing with it… that's how it happened, simple as that. It's fair enough and that, but I just wanted the truth about what had happened to my daughter, that was all.

Cafcass, the social services, the South West Surrey Assessment Team, they all accepted what she'd said. Nothing happened, but because I'd contacted social services about all this, she didn't turn up to the next contact as punishment. So that was her saying 'don't rock the boat or else'. And the authorities they just bought all this. "Father, just go away, shut up and don't say anything." That's the message.

In the meantime, I had a totally dismissive letter from Hedleys on April 25th. This was the first time they'd written to me since I'd taken the decision to represent myself and they came out all guns firing. They obviously thought that I was a bit of a div and that by talking down to me and using lots of legal terms they'd frighten me off. Grow up, I thought.

I wrote back on April 30th in a really calm and measured way. I was determined not to let them rattle me or make me say anything that I'd regret. Again I requested my family be allowed to see Sarah. "Your client denying my daughter any relationship with me I can understand as it follows suit with all the allegations and accusations against me. However, to deprive Sarah any contact with her only cousins and anyone at all from her father's family is ridiculous and unfair on all and is certainly not in her best interests." I asked for news regarding my possessions that were still at the house and, finally, that Jan turns up for contact on time and that she doesn't enter the room when Sarah and I were together. The last time we met, on April 27th, Jan came in the room when I was with Sarah and started harassing me and trying to provoke me. I didn't want that happening again.

*   *   *   *

On May 7th, Mrs Quinn, the Cafcass officer produced her "Welfare Report Concerning: Contact and Parental Responsibility". A twelve-page document.

For Mrs Quinn to write a report on how Sarah and I were together was a joke. She'd seen us together once at her office and how anyone can write a report of this nature based on one meeting is beyond me. This was an important document, one that was going to affect my life and Sarah's life and it as going to be based on one meeting?

For one thing, how can you judge how people are to-gether when you look at them in the contact centres? How can you be natural in these places? Also, it just so happened that this one time wasn't the best time for Sarah and me to be seen together. When Sarah was brought into the room where I was waiting for her she was crying and was visibly upset. Why was she crying? I've no idea. That's part of the thing about being there once a week and being denied the other six days and 22 hours. You don't know what's going on. Maybe she was unwell, maybe... Anything. I've got to be honest and say that I suspect Jan set the situation up. I'm not going to say anything particular because, unlike her, I don't make wild accusations without any proof or evidence, but think about it. I knew that Mrs Quinn was going to be there so I'm sure Jan knew. And it was in Jan's interests to show that Sarah had difficulty being with me, to show that we were crap together. So it wouldn't have been too hard to make sure that Sarah was upset. All she would have had to do was keep up her late last night or not let her have a sleep that morning or not give her enough food. Make a kid tired and, odds on, they'll be grumpy and cry.

Mrs Quinn said she'd mention that Sarah was upset when she came into the room in her report - but she didn't. "Due to Sarah's young age of 1 year and 4 months, I observed her with both parents separately. As indicated, she appeared comfortable and at ease in her mother's care. Sarah seemed generally unsettled during the time I saw her with her father and although he made every attempt to settle her she cried for the majority of the 30 minutes."

One thing that was nice to hear was that Mrs Macauly of Woking Contact Centre, said that, "Mr Chick is brilliant with the child. In Woking Contact Centre he is perfectly behaved."

The report was perfectly reasonable, perfectly calm – and completely in favour of Jan. They have a way of writing these things that makes it seem like they're being fair but really they're not. All the 'concerns' that Jan raised were highlighted. All the frustrations that I was feeling were over-looked. She wasn't called to account for any of her deceptions, wasn't questioned about all those contacts that had been missed. Whenever Jan had made an accusation about me being threatening or violent or abusive, it was mentioned, but mentioned without noting that there was no evidence or proof. Anyone reading it would have come to the conclusion that "where there's smoke there's fire". But really it was mud slinging and character slurs and that wasn't highlighted. If it had been fair or even-handed either the accusations would have been dismissed out of hand or they wouldn't have been mentioned at all.

Be honest, how easy would it have been for me to say that Jan had been making abusive calls to my mother? How easy would it have been for me to say any of things that she'd been saying about me? I could have played the same games as her – just like her, I didn't need any proof to do any of those things, I could have just said them – but I was a little more honest than that. I had a little bit more dignity than that. Strangely, none of this was mentioned in Mrs Quinn's report.

*   *   *   *

Meanwhile Hedleys were continuing to be aggressive and, to my mind, unreasonable. Yes, they were fighting her corner and I guess you'd expect them to be that way, but it was very difficult to deal with. No way were they interested in 'the child's best interests'. A letter dated May 12th states "Whilst our client finds attending the contact centre an inconvenience, she regards it as better than the alternative. Until you have calmed down and demonstrated to the court that there are better options that deal with proper concerns for Sarah, the contact centre appears to be the only appropriate venue."

Better options? A better option would be for their client

to turn up to the contact centres when she was supposed to. A better option would be for father and daughter to be allowed to have a relationship. "If you can satisfy the judge that you will behave reasonably and fairly the arrangements for building relationship with Sarah will improve." If I can behave reasonably and fairly? What about her also behaving reasonably and fairly?

There was the question of my property that was still at the house. "You should be aware that our client attempted to deal with that issue through your sister". Yes, I was aware of that. I was also aware that every time my sister suggested a date, Jan said it was inconvenient.

The next letter, three days later, said: "The Court has decided that we can be trusted to handle the sale (of your house) and that the sale can go ahead at £182,300 or greater. That was an interesting figure. £182,300. There had been an ongoing story about the sale of the house since we first split. We owned it jointly so we both had to agree to a sale. But it was Sarah's residence and she was Sarah's primary carer and her solicitors were getting involved.

The house story is a book in itself and there was plainly a story going on. The house had been valued by an independent estate agents – Mann & Co, the firm who sold us the house in the first place - at £199,950 the previous November. Now it was worth nearly twenty grand less? How did that happen? This was at a time when house prices around the country – and particularly in Surrey - were going through the roof, yet ours had gone down by £20,000? I'd found a buyer, a Mr Fisher, who offered £195,000. Was this accepted? Of course not. Jan wanted to sell the house to her friend for £182,300. Would it be too cynical for me to think that if the house were sold for less through her solicitors I would be entitled to less? And if, of course, she were to sell it to someone she knew...

It was so easy to get distracted in all this and there's a point during all this – and this is what was so frustrating about this whole story – where there's all this going on and it's just a distraction. You start to think, "Have it. Have the money, have the ladders, have the television cabinet, but let me see Sarah. If you'll be honest with me about all that, you can have anything." But she never could. All I want was the contact but the waters keep getting muddied by what was going on. And I think that that was what she wanted.

As I wrote to Hedleys, the main reason I was now acting for myself was because of the way I was represented at Reading Court. The Welfare Report based on the Findings of Fact hearing was misleading. The claims of abusive calls should have been thrown out of court because there was no evidence. The statement by Stuart Alexander stating that I had not threatened Jan outside the contact centre was returned because it was only initialled rather than signed. My lawyers should have picked up the fact that, as a member of contact staff, he was not allowed to sign any statements. But that should not have invalidated it. I was found guilty of violent behaviour but if I had been properly represented, no judge on Earth would have upheld that. "I have been behaving fairly and reasonably since before your client's vindictive behaviour began over six months ago. The sooner your client allows Sarah and I the proper unsupervised contact that every loving father and daughter are entitled to, the sooner we could stop wasting monies on solicitors, money which I would much rather spend on my daughter."

* * * *

I wrote to Hedleys on June 7th requesting that Mrs Quinn attends the final contact hearing on July 10th. I wanted to cross-examine her about that report. Why didn't she talk about Sarah being upset when she got there? There were other factual mistakes she made in that report and I wanted to talk to her about those and its general bias towards the mother.

I wanted to play a video of me and Sarah being together, so that the court could see how natural we were together, how much we still loved each other despite being denied so much time together. You know what they told me? They said that if I wanted to do this, I'd have to bring in my own television and video and set it all up myself. I mean. Come on. What sort of organisation is it that hasn't got those facilities? Was I the first person to ever have wanted to do something like that? I don't believe it. I just don't believe it.

I was being treated like a moron. I was being blocked at every level, and felt I was completely alone. I'd been to a Families Need Fathers meeting up in London, and they'd advised me about that final hearing, talked to me about how to approach it. They were nice enough blokes, you know, and obviously they've all got their stories and that. A lot of the blokes, obviously you can sympathise with them because they've all been screwed by the system, but what they were, it wasn't what I wanted to do. They've been sitting round talking for 10 or 20 years and what's changed? Nothing. They've got nothing changed. It's like a therapy group for them rather than trying something to get things moving. I don't want to be rude about them or anything, but it was a bit like a mother's meeting. It was just talk. Don't do anything. We'll be there to help you and support you. They advised me to have a McKenzie Friend with me. This means that, if you're representing yourself in court, you're entitled to have someone sit next to you. They can take notes, offer advice, but can't address the court directly. They're not meant to be a substitute for a solicitor. They are really just a fancy name for an assistant or friend to sit with you. But it's useful if you've never been in court before and need that bit of extra confidence or help.

What happened at that final hearing on July 10th? What happened was this: nothing. It was all the same noises, the same frustrations. I didn't get a chance to air my grievances, I didn't get a chance to question Mrs Quinn about her inaccurate and biased report... Nothing. What happened at that final hearing on July 10th was this. It gave the green light, yet again, to my ex to continue to deny and destroy my relationship with my daughter. Well, it would, wouldn't it? If you do something wrong and no one tells you that you mustn't do it, well that's the same as telling you to do it again.

So, unsurprisingly, Jan didn't bother to turn up to the contact centre on July 13. She didn't bother to turn up on July 20 either. Or July 27. She would have turned up on August 3, but Sarah was ill. So she couldn't. She must love these court hearings.

We were going nowhere, getting nowhere. I was writing letter after letter to Hedleys who ignored everything. I phoned and phoned and it was all "I'm sorry, they're not here." I left messages, no one phoned me back. I wondered if they would have a different attitude if I were a firm of solicitors instead of a lone bloke acting for himself. At the end of July I called Hedleys again, only to be told that they were no longer representing my former partner. On August 2, I wrote to the court complaining about this lack of contact. I would do all these things, but I knew it was all a bit of a waste of ink really.

CHAPTER ELEVEN

So what choice does a dad in my situation have? I hadn't seen Sarah for months, and the chances that I was going to see her were tiny. Every time Jan did something, or rather didn't do something like turn up to contact sessions, no one said or did anything. The courts, Cafcass – the authority that's supposed to be in charge of all this – nobody. Nobody did anything. And meanwhile I suffered.

In July she told the court that she wouldn't be able to bring Sarah to two contacts because she was going on holiday. But I know that she only went away for one week. Okay, you might think that's a small thing, one week, but it was typical. Her taking the piss, no one checking, no one caring – and me losing out.

On August 10, my ex again phoned in saying that she wouldn't be coming to the contact. Because – of course – Sarah was ill. But you know the thing that really got to me was that she stated she rang the contact centre at Woking when that week's contact was supposed to be at Guildford. That's how much she cared about being there. That's how seriously she took the whole business. Me? Those two hours were my whole week, for her it didn't matter, she didn't care, she wasn't going to go and she didn't care who knew it.

So I said enough's enough. I'm not going to do it anymore. I'm not going to go to the contacts anymore. Every week I went, every week I waited, every week I went home, disappointed. I can't tell you about the heartache that caused. Each week, sitting there at home, waiting, thinking about the coming Saturday, getting really excited and nervous and everything in between. And every week coming back home, totally deflated, totally let down. Angry, hurt, disappointed, upset… pick your own words. And, you know I felt really good about myself for having made that decision. That didn't last.

It's all very well being noble and that, saying that you're not going to subject yourself or your kids to this torture anymore. It's all very well thinking that, you know, I'm behaving properly and it's all them that are the sadistic lying bastards or whatever – but at the end of the day I'm not seeing Sarah and she's not seeing me. However bad the contact centre system is, it's all there is and if I want to see Sarah that's what I've got to do. The idea that I'm not going to see her at all is doing my head in. Again, the father finds himself over a barrel. What can he do? Nothing.

So on August 12 I rang Mrs Macauly (the co-ordinator of Woking Contact Centre) and told her. I said I wanted contact as basically something was better than nothing and as I sat there on the end of the phone, thinking about everything from all the missed contacts that we were supposed to have had to how the ex was going to be laughing because she's basically won again to what the reality actually was – me waiting at the contact centre and her phoning in at the last minute saying Sarah wasn't coming in for a variety of invented reasons like she was ill… as I was thinking about that, Mrs Macauly said, "Sorry, but you can't change your mind because the place was now taken." What?

That was new. I didn't know that was going to happen. Basically they have a capacity for a certain amount of dads and children and there's a long waiting list. What I didn't realise was that while I was moaning about what a rubbish system it was, how abusive it was and how unnatural it was, while I was doing all that there were a thousand dads who would have killed to be in my situation. I was one of the lucky ones. That's a laugh, isn't it? By the time I'd had my change of heart about whether I wanted to go to the contact centre, they'd given my place away and now I was one of those thousand dads. So there's me, one of the lucky dads, who has a chance to see his daughter once a week, taking up a valuable space, and Jan is flagrantly flouting the law. Not turning up. And there's another dad who'd have killed for that contact session, whose ex may have brought his kid, who may have seen his kid. So not only is she depriving me and Sarah of seeing each other, but some other dad and his kid.

And the courts did nothing about her deliberate waste of contact centre time.

By now I'd lost all hope that the authorities, that the system, would do something. They so clearly didn't care. I'd long given up any hope that my ex would behave like a human being (if not to me, then to her daughter) but now I knew that not only would she continue to behave like the lying, cheating thing that she was, but also the system would support her every step of the way.

And would I ever get to see Sarah? No – because Sarah was ill. Sure.

It was coming up to a year since I split with Jan and she started her campaign to wipe Sarah out of my life. I'd done everything right and she'd done everything wrong and it just got to the stage where I said enough's enough. I was doing it the way you're meant to do it, the way the law says you're supposed to do it and I was getting shafted at every angle. I was losing out and, more importantly, my daughter was losing out. Well, she couldn't do anything about it but I could.

There was no longer any possibility of compromise. I'd tried that, I'd tried doing what they told me to do. And every time I did what they told me to do, Jan would twist the knife, the system would support her and I got shafted. And when

I say I got shafted. I mean Sarah got shafted. I couldn't see her, but also she couldn't see me. What sort of State is it that denies a child their parent? To compromise meant doing nothing and making more solicitors rich. Compromising meant sitting back and saying "OK". Compromising meant giving in. And I was done giving in. If they wanted me to give up my daughter… forget it. There was no way I was going to do that.

I knew that I had two choices: I could lie down and be walked over by everyone. Or I could do something about it. And I'd been lying down long enough. Now it was time to go outside the system.

PART TWO

CHAPTER TWELVE

You go outside the system because you recognise that the system has become the problem. It's an act of desperation, something you do when you've tried everything else. You do what you've been told to do, you've tried being a good boy and it doesn't do any good. I knew that if I just carried on the way I'd been nothing would change. Jan wouldn't change. Why should she? She'd been ignoring the court orders – effectively breaking the law – and no one ever said anything to her. Why would she change her attitude now? The solicitors wouldn't change. Or the only time they would change was when I'd run out of money. There were only two things that would change: me and Sarah. I'd change by getting depressed and frustrated. And Sarah would change in every way – only I wouldn't be there to see it.

It's easy enough to make a decision like "Now I'm going to go outside the system", but what do you actually do? One thing I didn't want to do was anything violent or anything that could be called violent. That would be playing right into her hands and would give them ammunition to say things like, "There, told you he was a violent man." I wasn't going to fall for that. I wasn't going to become the person that she said I was. I'd have no chance of seeing Sarah then.

You can do almost anything but you want to make sure it's big and bold, that it's going to be noticed, that the message and the idea will get across. And don't take this wrong, but the question of whether, strictly speaking, it was legal… Well, was what they were doing to me, was that legal? Basically if you protest on the ground, people can walk past you. Have a glance, a bit of a little glimpse and that's it. I wanted to do something that was big, something that was as big as I could do.

There's not many things you can do without the authorities and the police coming and arresting you or – worse - just ignoring you. Where did the idea for a crane come from? I don't honestly recall, I don't know how the idea came to me. I was doing a bit of driving at the time and was just looking around, thinking of what sort of protest I could do, and driving around Victoria I saw this huge crane. I looked at it and it was such a big, kinda imposing thing, I thought, "That'll do." What I felt at the time – and what I know now – is that if you're up there then you're in control. You start when you want to start, you end it when you want to end it. The police aren't going to come up there and try and drag you down. It was the only bit of control I had in my life because everything else I had no control. So I was going to do my protest about this fucking scandal, about these state sponsored kidnappers, and it was going to end when I chose to end it.

I took that thought away with me and let it sit there for a few days but the more I thought about it, the more it made sense. Bang in the middle of London, this huge metal structure. No one's going to miss that. The whole idea appealed to me and, contrary to some of the things that have been written about me I haven't got a problem with heights. Nothing like that.

I went back a few days later to have a look around and see what I'd need to get in and get up and I was surprised to see that there was nothing. No security guards or guard dogs or nothing. You've got a big structure like that in the middle of town and any Tom can basically stroll up and climb it.

At 9pm on August 23 I went up and, to be honest, it wasn't

much of a protest. It was my first one like and I hadn't really thought it through properly. I wasn't up as Spiderman at this stage, it wasn't nearly that organised. That whole thing was still a long way off. I took some food, a few Mars bars and bread rolls. Not many clothes because it was quite warm anyway and some bottles of water. I took about four or five banners which were just spray-painted slogans about basic rights and discrimination. Really Mickey Mouse compared to the later ones I did. You live and learn.

When I did that first one, like I say, I didn't have much of a clue about anything. Well, I don't suppose you do the first time you do something. I didn't even have an idea of how long I was going to stay up there. I suppose when I went up there I was thinking about two or three days, something along those lines, but it wasn't until I was up there that I realised what it was all about. I could see people looking up, but basically I was so high up that no one could read the banners. I could barely see the people down on the ground, and I knew that they were there. How on earth could they see me when probably they didn't even know I was there? Even if they could see me, there was no way they could have read those banners. It dawned on me that it wasn't really doing anything.

It was, to be truthful, a fantastic feeling up there. You feel really powerful in a way because no one can touch you, no one can tell you what to do. You're just there by yourself, sitting there with your own thoughts and nothing else. It's fantastically quiet too. All that noise that's always going on around you – the constant noise of people talking, the noise of traffic, of things happening, there's nothing like that up there. It's a bit freaky in that sense, but once you get used to it, it's really peaceful. The other thing it was really boring. Really boring. It sounds obvious but there's nothing to do. Once I'd got up there and there was the excitement of that done, what else was there? I'd unfolded all the banners, got everything set up and... then what? Sit and wait for something to happen, and I can't remember what I thought but nothing was going to happen up there. If this was going to achieve anything it would happen down below, after I'd come down.

I was sat up there and as soon as I realised what the story was there was a kind of feeling of "Fuck, what do I do now?" It was a Bank Holiday weekend and there was hardly anyone around. There were a few fellers working, doing a bit of work on the site, and they noticed me up there.

Whenever I talk to people about the crane protests that I've done they always ask me two things. Where do I sleep and how do I deal with some of your more basic functions – where do I piss and shit. Everyone always wants to know that. It's all really easy. I sleep up there in the driver's seat. To be honest, there are better places to sleep but there are also worse. It's not so bad. It's not somewhere you'd pay to go on holiday, but you've got to remember I ain't doing this for the good of my health or because there's nothing on the telly. Going up a crane 200 feet in the air isn't something you do because you're bored – it's something you do because you're desperate and you've run out of alternatives. You've tried the more normal stuff and it doesn't help. So when you run out of the normal stuff, you get desperate.

Going to the lav is easy as well. I took up a few water bottles because of all the things you need, probably water is the most important. As soon as you finish a bottle, well there's your lav. And as for having a dump, it's not pretty but everyone's got to do it. There isn't a person alive, there isn't an animal on the planet that doesn't shit and, you know, most of them just get on with it. Bags. Plastic bags. That's what I used. And no, I didn't throw my shit down on people or throw it at coppers or anything like that.

Days passed up there and nothing was happening. One of the fellers who was doing security had a word with me. He said that it was Bank Holiday weekend and if I stayed up there he'd have to stay there as well and it would mess his whole weekend up. Just another bloke trying to get by. What can you do? So basically I agreed to come down. So I did a deal with him.

That weekend it was my mate's 40th birthday and there was a whole gang of my mates going to the dogs for a night out. So I said to the security bloke, I'm going to come down now, disappear for a bit. You can do what you like. And that's what I did. I got my stuff together and went down. I went off to the dogs with my mates, had a bit of a night out, and then when it was all finished... I went back to the crane and went back up so that when they all came back in on Monday it was like I'd never been away. It was no big deal, like.

I went up on the Friday and by the next Wednesday I'd had enough. I realised that it wasn't really doing any good – it wasn't doing any anything and, though it was a big deal to me, it was no big deal to the rest of the world. I was just sitting up there and the rest of the world was getting on with its business. In terms of doing any good it was a total non-event. Like I say, apart from my brother the only people who knew I was up there were a couple of coppers and the blokes on the site. There was no press, no nothing.

When I came down the fellers from the site took me round to their canteen and bought me breakfast. They were sympathetic to my cause and because I'd been straight with them, they were straight with me. They could see that I was just an ordinary bloke who was a bit desperate and at his wits end. The law? Nothing. They didn't rally care either. As I walked out of the site there were a couple of coppers there and they just basically said, "Don't do that again, will you?"

How did I do at the dogs? No good.

CHAPTER THIRTEEN

All the reasons why I did that first crane protest didn't go away. I went up that thing, stayed there for five days and came down again and nothing changed. I still wasn't seeing Sarah. The ex still wasn't turning up to the contacts – she must have been loving all this. All my possessions were still caught up at her house – and she was still denying me access to them, still denying that she had them at all. I couldn't work because all my stuff was there, I couldn't get any money because I couldn't work. The solicitors weren't doing anything to help – they just weren't doing anything at all except taking what money I'd already given them. And then the one asset I did have – the house that we'd bought together – then that was gone.

It didn't take any great thought, I knew what I had to do. I had to do the protest again, but this time I had to do it right, I had to make sure that people knew what was going on.

On September 7th, I started my second crane protest. This time I found a smaller crane, something that people would be able to see. Last time I thought that the bigger the crane was thee better it would be. This time I knew different. I found a crane in Guildford, nearer where I lived. It wasn't so high, the banners were better – and no, I still wasn't dressed up as Spiderman. This one was nowhere near as the crane in Victoria, it was only about 100ft high. (Still only about 100ft high? You try going up 100ft in the sky. See what that feels like). The one in Victoria was about 200 ft plus – maybe 250ft - but only half as high as the London eye, but we'll come to that.

This protest didn't last too long because, basically, I was conned. I went up at 6pm on the 7th and at 9.30am on the 9th I was approached by a police negotiator. He seemed a reasonable bloke and we talked for a while about who I was and what I was doing and what I hoped to achieve by all this. I thought this was something positive, that something might actually happen. The negotiator said that if I came down peacefully there and then they'd look into my case and look into all the crimes that had been committed against me. That was what I'd been hoping for. Going up that crane did work. I was going to get taken seriously. Someone would listen and maybe – just maybe – bring that… bring my ex to justice.

Was it fuck. That police negotiator wasn't a copper at all. It was a freelance journalist pretending to be a copper hoping to get a story. Bastard.

As soon as I came down I was nicked. The police couldn't have me come down and not do anything about it so they nicked me on suspicion. Suspicion of nicking my own ladder and the camera I'd recently been allowed to collect from Jan's. It was all bollocks. It was my stuff – they knew that. They had to do something because you can't be seen to get away with it. It's all for show, like. If they let me get away with it, they'll have every Tom, Dick or Superman running up and down cranes every minute.

A few hours after they'd done their 'investigation' I was bailed. "You are bailed to appear at Guildford police station on October 14th in relation to the alleged offence suspicion of theft. Notice is hereby given that you are no longer required to surrender to bail on the time and the date shown but this does not preclude the continued investigation of the alleged offence or any subsequent action against you."

Yeah, whatever. There was no case. Just the police being the police.

Actually when I was talking to the coppers it did seem like the police had a reasonable handle on it. It was all basically about two bitter people fighting about custody. There was no theft, there was no assault, nothing. But to save face they've still got to arrest you and have a go at you. They arrested me for being up a crane basically, but they did seem to know that the rest was bullshit because there was no charge. But then again, there couldn't have been because there was no evidence of anything ever. Never was. Never has been.

Still I wasn't seeing Sarah.

*   *   *   *

On September 28 2002 we had the first contact for 12 weeks at Guildford, the only contact centre we could go to because there still wasn't room at Woking. Jan arrived 40 minutes late. Forty minutes might not seem much but after three months of nothing – three months of going, waiting, hoping, three months of frustration and disappointment, three months of despair that it would ever end, that it wouldn't become four months or five months – after all this, believe me, 40 minutes is a lifetime. Each minute you think, "Is she coming? Will I see her?"

She arrived 40 minutes late. I think the excuse that day was a puncture. Whatever. Who cares? She could have said she'd been abducted by aliens for all I cared. Probably it would have been as close to the truth as well, but like I say, who cares?

Seeing Sarah again was fantastic. Fantastic and heartbreaking. Have you any idea how much a little kid changes in three months? A little girl basically a year and a half old? The changes are enormous and you just sit there and look at this little girl whose life is flying by and whose life, really, you've got nothing to do with. Who are her friends? I don't know. They don't come to the contact centre. What are their names? What does she do with them? What are their parents like? I don't know any of these things, the normal things any normal parent knows... I don't know them. I'm the bloke who spends his life up a crane because he doesn't know any of these things.

Contact was lovely. Just seeing her was lovely. For her? I don't know. I can't imagine sitting in some "prison" with a bloke who she knows less and less would have been much fun. Kids like running around and playing and being out there and stuff, not sitting in some grey place with me. That's true, but we've got to grab all the time we can. Every week that passes when we don't see each other at all is another week closer to her forgetting who I am completely. And that, I guess, is what the ex was aiming for. But I wasn't going to let that happen. This is my daughter and I was going to fight for her.

The contact was supposed to be from 2.30pm till 4.30pm, but the place actually shuts at five, so I ran up that extra 30 minutes at the end, so I only ended up 10 minutes short. Ten minutes and three months. No, make that ten minutes and 18 months.

I decided to re-employ Mahany & Co as it was my only hope of progressing matters. Every letter I sent myself, she just ignored. On October 9th, Mahany received a letter from her solicitors. They were complaining about the fact that I decided to cancel the contact and then changed my mind and decided to ask for it to be reinstated. They knew full well the reasons why I wanted to cancel it and why it wanted it back but they didn't care about any of that. Those feelings, they were all about being a human being and having feelings like a human being – nothing they knew about.

Their letter said: "I feel that we have been messed around enough already with this refusal to attend then a change of heart. The inconsistency of Mr Chick's commitment to attend sessions with his daughter has caused upset to my family and me..."

My inconsistency? OK, well at least I couldn't accuse her of inconsistency. She was consistent all right, consistent with her lies and evasions. I knew from the tone of this letter that the chances of there being any contact in the near future were zero. And sure enough...

October 19th. Jan can't make it to the contact.

October 26th. Sarah's ill.

November 4th. I get a call from the centre saying that Jan can't make it to the contact.

November 9th. Sarah's ill.

Does it make you want to scream? It did me. Why was no one picking up on any of this? Why was no one taking any notice? What's Mrs Macauly doing at this time? Apparently there was some problem with Jan attending the Guildford centre but that was fine because a space had become available at the Woking centre. But then Jan said she couldn't make it to Woking until the end of November. Because... There was no because. No reason. And no one asked. What was going on?

All this "Sarah's ill" was doing my head in. Listen. I was the bad parent, the drug abusing, aggressive violent out-of-control maniac who couldn't be trusted with the welfare of my daughter, but this Sarah's ill business... what's that all about?

You'd think things like that would have alerted the authorities. Rewind back to the beginning and remember that quote – it's "in the child's best interests". You'd think that they'd wonder about that. You'd think they might wonder about a parent who didn't know which contact centre to go to. You'd look at a child who can't make the contact because she was ill so often and wonder whether that child was being looked after properly.

What sort of parent was she? Why was Sarah ill so often? Was there some real problem with her health? If so, why didn't she take her to a doctor and get it sorted out? Had there ever been any medical evidence of this ongoing illness? Of course not. Did anyone ever ask for any proof or evidence? Of course not. Was she being looked after properly? Didn't sound like it. Was her diet right? Was she getting the right foods and vitamins? Didn't sound like it. Was she being looked after properly? Was she getting exercise, fresh air, and all the things that a normal kid needs to grow up healthily? Didn't sound like it.

It didn't sound to me that Jan was being a very good mother. To be honest, it was doing my head in. Forget all the stuff about imagine how all this would go down if it were me who was coming up with all those excuses. Forget all the stuff about how I would be slated and slagged off if a kid in my care were so ill so often. (And can you imagine the fuss Jan would kick up if I were looking after Sarah and she was ill so often).

Regardless of whether they thought that the mother was lying or anything, even if they thought that she was a great person and the father was a terrible person, even if the authorities were paying attention even a little bit, they've got to ask how come a little kid like that is ill so much?

They've never challenged anything she's ever said. They've not required evidence of anything she's ever said. All the lies add on to themselves and mount up and it's shocking that nowhere along the line did anyone say, "Hang about. Something here isn't right. Either this kid has got some serious medical condition or that mother is taking the piss big time."

Is all this being missed because she's a mother and mothers can do no wrong? Is it being missed because the system's so rubbish and all the people working in it are so incompetent? I don't know. Probably a mixture of every-thing, a bit of everything. The thing is, the contact centres, they're just volunteers trying to help fathers and children out, they're not linked to Cafcass or the court. They don't have to tell the court of one's turned up or one hasn't.

One question though – and I don't want to have a go at them, but if the people who work at the centres are volunteers, wouldn't they have noticed? The idea of a 'volunteer' is of someone who does something because they care, not because they have to and if they care… you'd have thought nice caring person would have noticed something like this. I'm not having a go at them, but after Sarah's been ill 15 times or something, you'd have thought they might have noticed.

But that's the problem. One of the problems. They're there to supervise contact. That's their job. They're not there to report on who's there or anything. In fairness to them they must be snowed under with work. Think about it. There's no room here or there, people are sitting on waiting lists, waiting for a vacancy so that they can sit down and see their kid so you can imagine how busy they are. And they've got no training, no expertise. It's not them I'm questioning, it's the system.

The truth about Sarah's illness is that she had some strange disease that only hit her on Saturday afternoons. The rest of the time she was fine. It's an increasingly common disease that seems to affect children of separated parents who don't get on with each other and who are under the care of Cafcass. It's called denyfatheritis.

Mrs Macauly at Woking was OK actually. There was some feedback from her, when I attended and all that. But Guildford, they never said a word. They wouldn't confirm or deny whether my ex had turned up or whether Sarah was ill or if she was late, not a word. And why not? What difference to them? It's not their job, not their concern, not their problem. Next.

It had been a month since our last contact and, looking back, I should have known something was going to happen. It always happens, another little something, a complaint, an allegation, an accusation, anything that puts the attention on me and stops people looking at her and her disgraceful record of not attending the contacts. Sure enough…

On October 29th, I got a letter from Mahany saying they'd had a phone call from Miss Green.

"She took Sarah out this afternoon. Sarah got to the car before she did and it was smeared with dog excrement. Sarah put her fingers in this and wiped it on her clothing and put it in her mouth and hair. She has become ill. Miss Green is convinced you are the perpetrator of this deed and I get the impression that she intends to take it further. She is not well disposed towards you to say the least. Apparently a neighbour saw a tall shaven-headed person in the area".

Not well disposed towards me? That's funny, because as it happens, I'm not well disposed towards her. What a sick bastard story. What a really sick thing to dream up. Did it happen? Of course it didn't happen. I suppose it might have happened but if it did it had nothing to do with me. But if had happened... where was the medical report? Where was the doctor's report? Where was the neighbour? As ever... nothing. Just wild accusations and no proof. Still, it's another little notch on the "Dave's a mad bastard" register.

It was a rubbish story. At this stage I didn't even know where she lived. It was nonsense. It did make me wonder why she would be happy to let a kid, not yet two-years-old, run out to the road by herself, no one holding her hand or anything. A child of that age, shouldn't someone have been looking after her a bit better? Of course, no one questioned it, no one picked up on it.

On November 9th I got a letter in the post telling me that Jan had moved and this was Sarah's new address. Who sent it? Don't know. It didn't have any information apart from just the basic story and the new address. I was happy to get it – I always think it's nice to know where your daughter's living – but I don't care who sent it. It could even have been Jan in a moment of concern and humanity. Forget that. It was more likely to have been the Tooth Fairy.

A month later – to give her some credit. She was getting very precise about all this - there was another mad letter, this time on November 22nd.

"On the evening of November 19th I left my parents house to attend work at 18.00. At 20.00 my mother and daughter went to put milk bottles out on the doorstep. My mother opened the door to find a dead fox on the doorstep that had been sliced open. Its intestines were hanging out. Both her and my daughter screamed, my daughter was shouting 'Doggy'." Then there's the usual stuff about "Mr Chick has in the past been admitted to psychiatric hospital..." Before you even ask, no, I didn't. I might hate her but I haven't got an argument with any foxes. Jan stated that I rang her mum that evening saying I'd "left something outside". If this was true, surely Sarah wouldn't have been allowed out to be the first one to see what it was.

It's a bullshit story, just like the dog shit story. Bullshit. These two horrible things happen and, both times, Sarah just happens to be there. At Jan's house and at Jan's mother's house, Sarah just happend to be there.

A few days later I thought I'd call the RSPCA to see if Jan had reported it to them. They said she did, but when they went round to her mum's house, there was no sign of anything. No dead fox. No intestines. No blood. Maybe the fox made a miraculous recovery and ran off.

You know the really odd thing about both those stories? Listen, all Jan had to do was say to the police that I'd threatened her. No proof, no evidence, we know all that. If she wanted to have a go at me or just keep me from thinking we might be making progress, that's all she needed. A quick call and the cops and the system would do the rest. But here she was, coming up with these strange stories about dog shit and dead foxes. Maybe she was simply bored with the usual "Dave's threatened me" story. (I know I was). Maybe she was just testing the system, seeing what level of bullshit they'd buy.

I decided to hire Hamnet Osborne Tisshaw of Haywards Heath. I'd had a little contact with them a month earlier and they seemed to be on the ball. Mahany & Co? There was too much water under the bridge for that one. They'd not taken me where I wanted to be, and we were still messing about trying to get Jan to even attend a contact. I needed someone to be a bit... harder.

Hamnet's first letter out sounded good. "We enclose a schedule of the contact visits up to February 22, 2003. You will note that the next contact session is on Saturday November 16, 2002 at the Woking Contact Centre. Please can you kindly ensure that you adhere to the schedule? We should advise you that if you do not make Sarah available for contact on these dates, we will have no hesitation in making immediate application to the court and you will be held in contempt of court for such a breach of the order." Sounded tough.

Hamnets inform me that Jan was now going to represent herself because after spending £20,000 so far she can't afford the solicitors any longer. She also said she's unable to afford to provide for Sarah and that her parents are having to provide clothing and food. £20,000? Bollocks. And even if she did spend a few bob, what was she spending it on? Denying me Sarah, denying Sarah me and attempting to destroy any future relationship between us. Well, that's money well spent.

I'd say something like "Maybe she could have taken a few quid out of that twenty grand to look after Sarah properly, buy her some proper healthy food, so she wouldn't be ill so often" but people would think I'm being sarcastic.

Strangely – well I find this strange – five days later there was an upturn in the cleaning business and things got suddenly much better. So much so that she had a new driveway laid which, I later found out, cost £2,000. Well, I'm glad that she's had such a rapid turnaround in her fortunes and that things are so much better now. Well, good for her. Maybe now she'll be able to feed and clothe Sarah herself and not have to rely on her parents like she's just said. Maybe Sarah will get some better food and stuff and won't be ill so often, maybe... (Just in case there really is some sympathy, Jan's now employing 17 people and driving a new 4x4 that just cost over £20,000).

What a lot of old bollocks. Does she expect anyone to believe any of this? It's all lies, just her saying any old rubbish because she knows by now – like I do – that nothing she says will ever be checked up on, nothing will ever be looked at. No one will ask for any proof of anything. It's all lies. The only concrete thing is the new driveway.

CHAPTER FOURTEEN

Still, the threats and abuse continued – had something I'd said rattled her? Maybe that letter from Hamnets did do some good. Or was she really now acting alone and without the advice of a solicitor? Was that why she'd started saying such blatantly stupid things?

The next thing – predictably - is that she's complained to the courts that I was making abusive and threatening phone calls to her. Again, it came to nothing because there were no abusive and threatening phone calls. She does all these things, makes all these claims and then if the police or the courts or whoever it is ever say "And where's the proof?" she disappears. Because there's never any proof, there's never any evidence. It's all just part of this campaign to make people think that Sarah's dad is a bad man, that he's not to be trusted. That he's not to be trusted with his daughter. It trips itself up at every turn but no-one picks up on it and the bullshit "Sarah's ill" stories just keep coming out and the bad man – that's me – doesn't get to see his daughter.

It's not subtle and it's not smart. This time she said she was so concerned about these abusive calls that she was going to have a BT trace operating system installed on her phone line and her parents' phone line. What would she do next time she complained of threatening and abusive phone calls?

It didn't take so long to find out. On January 7th the phone went. It was DC Foote of Guildford police. He said

that Jan had made an allegation that I'd been making abusive calls to her. Again. Apparently when she tried to check
the number by phoning 1471 the number was withheld. But
this wasn't a problem for Jan because, remember, she had
the BT trace mechanism and that would nail that nasty bastard Dave Chick. As it happened, both Jan and the coppers
forgot to activate the trace mechanism that she'd had put
on her phone to track all my abusive phone calls. Yeah, right.

DC Foote stated in his report: "On this occasion it would
appear that Ms Green didn't enter a 4 digit pin number into
her phone that would have activated the trace mechanism."
Isn't that convenient! Why would you go to all the trouble
of having this trace mechanism installed and then when the
very thing that you're trying to trace happens… you forget
to press the buttons? Isn't that convenient? What's more
likely is that there weren't any abusive phone calls, nothing
happened. Nothing happened, no proof of anything, no
evidence, no nothing. In the real world, the world where
there's justice and where people are treated equally and
without State prejudice, she'd be done for wasting police
time. Isn't that what it's called? Making false allegations.
But no. Again, the result of all this absolute lying bullshit is
that the police had to get in touch with me. And that would
go on their records and, again, it looks as though Dave Chick
is the bad man.

The thing was, I was in Yorkshire at the time, a fact that
was confirmed by the police who checked it out with the
people I was staying with. I suppose you could say any
number of things. I could have gone to a phone box and
made the calls from there. I could have got a mate to call her
on my behalf. Really, in truth I could have done anything if
I'd have wanted to, but the fact is that I didn't make any
abusive calls. Why would I? Why would I risk everything
by doing something so stupid? I wouldn't.

Forgot to activate the trace mechanism. What bollocks.

I hadn't seen Sarah for eight weeks now – she'd been ill,

remember? – and I requested a contact hearing at Reading Court to try and sort the situation out. It was plainly ridiculous and she needed to be reminded by the legal system that she couldn't abuse us all like she'd been doing. What happened next was maybe the most outrageous thing in this whole story. Or maybe it's just typical. Whatever it is, it gives you a fantastic insight onto how the legal system views the complaints of fathers and the complaints of mothers – and whose side they come down on.

Contact was supposed to take place at Woking on December 7th. Hamnets sent out a letter on December 5th reminding her. "Our client instructs us that the Contact Centre have been in communication with you to remind you that there is a contact session due on December 5th. We again remind you of the order made by His Honour Judge Critchlow on July 10th 2002 which provides for weekly contact." Meanwhile, I filed a complaint against Dafydd Griffiths, the barrister who'd failed me at Reading Court in March. I had already filed a complaint against Mahany & Co with The Law Society. I don't know about the solicitors, but for me this was a full-time occupation.

Hamnets sent out letter after letter. "We understand that, yet again, you failed to make Sarah available for contact on…" Eventually, they applied for the court to set "an urgent directions appointment" and we were granted a date: December 18th at 10am. "Time allowed: 30 minutes." The bad news was that we were up in front of His Honour Judge Critchlow, and me coming up against Judge Critchlow was always going to be a complete waste of time. They booked me a barrister, Miss Aviva Le Provost. Maybe I'd stand a better chance of justice if I had a female barrister. The hearing had all the hallmarks of a Judge Critchlow story. We went there and presented our cases.

The judge listened to all this, heard all the "Sarah's ill" excuses and you know what he said? He said to Jan, "If it's hard for you to get there once a week, we'll make it once a fortnight so you can comply with the order." I couldn't believe it. It was if nothing made any sense. How could he come to a decision like that? How could it be? I'd wanted the court hearing because I wanted to see Sarah and Jan was taking the piss. The judge listened to all the evidence and then ordered contact to be reduced by 50%. Lovely man. That's not all. He also granted Jan's request that contact be changed from 2.30-4.30pm to 3-5pm. It doesn't sound like much difference, does it? But it was actually a bastard thing to do. When she did bother to turn up, on those few occasions, she was nearly always late. Well, the contact centres close at 5pm and I could make up my lost time in tha half hour at the end between 4.40pm and 5pm. But this way… there was no slack. If she was late I lost out on that time and there would be no way to get it back. It was a cheap, childish thing to do. Typical of the woman.

I don't think the lovely Judge Critchlow liked me very much. Certainly he didn't like the idea of dads standing up to be counted. The other thing he did was this. The cost of the psychiatrist was to have been split between us. He ordered that I'd have to bear the whole cost myself. Two grand. Why did he do this? Why did he do any of it? Not a nice man.

As we were about to leave his court, he declared that the next hearing wasn't going to be held until February 2004 – 13 months away. Whatever happened to the idea that cases re "child involved" are subject to a minimal delay?

Judge Critchlow. He's off my Christmas card list. For good.

CHAPTER FIFTEEN

New year and still the situation continues. Sarah's birthday came and went and the nearest I got to celebrating it with her was sending a card. Did she get it? I don't know. Was she told about it? I don't know. What did she look like? What was her favourite TV programme? Her favourite food? What about her teeth? How many did she have now? I didn't know. I didn't know any of the answers to these questions or any other questions. Slowly... slowly it seemed as though she was fading from view. I was determined that that wouldn't happen. I was determined that Jan wouldn't get her way, that I wouldn't be wiped from Sarah's life.

My whole life was on hold because of this situation. This seemed like my full time job, my occupation and it was awful. It was my full time occupation and I was no nearer getting anything. I had mates and I went out with them and that, but even they were starting to get bored with me banging on about this story the whole time. People can like you as much as anything but they only want to hear about the sad stuff for so long. They've all got their own lives with their own problems and things to deal with.

The other thing was, being with my mates who had kids and a happy family life was starting to make me feel sad. It wasn't like I begrudged them any of that, it was just that it made me think about my own situation more. I'd be out doing whatever I was doing and not thinking about Sarah and the whole story particularly and if I bumped into someone I knew who was out and about with their kids, it would just throw me back into thinking about it all. I wasn't jealous of them – OK, maybe I was jealous a bit. I didn't want them not to have it. I just wanted what was mine. Again the question hit me: what had I done to deserve this?

While all this is going on, guess what. We've had only 46 hours of contact out of the 94 hours that should have happened. Out of the last 50 possible hours of 'contact' with my little girl, we've had only 12. So there's all this bullshit about non-existent abusive calls but what it's really all about is making people forget about the fact that she's not complying with the contact order. And, fair play to her, it's working. The law doesn't care that she's breaking it. The law does nothing about it.

I've missed Sarah's second birthday. I've missed her growing and developing. I've missed her learning how to walk and how to talk. I've missed her growing up. That is what all the bullshit is about. That ex of mine making sure that all those things have nothing to do with me.

What's that line in the family law? In the child's best interests. Oh yes.

*   *   *   *

On February 3rd, 2003, we had – and sit down now because this is the shocking bit – a contact. I was beginning to think that this sort of thing wasn't going to ever happen again, but – and I don't know why – it did. Maybe she came to this contact just to taunt me, because this was the hardest contact I'd ever been to.

Sarah was over two years old now, and at the age where she was understanding more words. And that, I'm sure, was what was going on here. Every time I'd seen her in the past, she was perfect. This time was different. Where before she'd been happy and loving and playful, full of cuddles and kisses, this time she was upset and wary and scared.

On one hand I could understand it. She hadn't seen me

for ages. Who was I? What was she doing here with this strange man? And – and this is what really freaked me out – what had she been hearing about me? What had she been told? Sure as hell I knew that she wouldn't have been told what a nice man I was. It was the saddest hour or so of my life. My little girl acting like she didn't know who I was. Worse, she was acting like she did know who I was – and she didn't like it.

The next contact meeting – yes, there was another one – was easier. Sarah was closer, more trusting. After we'd been together for an hour or so, I leaned over and said to her,

"Daddy loves Sarah. Doesn't Sarah love Daddy anymore?"

Sarah looked at me in that way that kids look when they don't know what to say. She didn't say anything.

"Is everything OK?" I said to her. She looked at me, you know, like she didn't know what to say. I had a funny feeling about what had been going on. I didn't want to say it but I knew I had to. So I said to her, "Does Mummy say that Daddy's nasty?"

She just looked at me and, very quietly, said, "Yep".

That was the last contact we had for 21 months.

*   *   *   *

I can't tell you how that made me feel. It was my worst nightmare come true, something I'd thought about but never really wanted to think about. Jan had Sarah all week, every week. All she needed to do was, every so often, drop in a word about me. She didn't have to bang Sarah over the head with it, she just had to very slowly, very gently tell Sarah what she wanted to. God knows what sort of poison she'd been fed. Daddy's a monster? Daddy hates you? Daddy doesn't care about you? I don't know. She could have been told anything and I wouldn't put it past my ex to tell her anything.

And the truth was, I'd seen Sarah so infrequently that what we'd had no real time or space or opportunity to build up a proper relationship. Her mother was the one who she had a relationship with if her mother said that we don't live with Daddy because Daddy is a nasty man... What chance did the truth stand?

It added to the sense of desperation I felt, the sense of isolation.

On March 15th I was meant to have contact. Instead I got a call on the 14th telling me that Sarah was ill. No way! Sarah was ill? She's normally in such good health. Especially during that contact time of the month. Ho hum. I don't know why – really, I can't begin to imagine why – but I didn't believe it. So I did something that the courts wouldn't have approved of, something that I knew I'd get into trouble for, but it was something I just had to do. You see, when I do something that's against the law – or against what the law has told me to do – I don't mess around with bullshit abusive phone calls like I've been accused of. I do something a bit more... constructive. In order to find out, I had to spy on them

I went round to Jan's house and parked a discrete distance away. I sat in my car and waited. I saw Jan come out of the house with Sarah. I kept a distance – we've all seen it done in the films and it's really not so hard to do in real life - and saw her drop Sarah off at her mum's. Not the doctors? How strange. Then I followed my ex to an office she was cleaning in Bookham, Surrey. Enough was enough. OK, I shouldn't have done it but I did. I was so frustrated by all this and I just wanted to get some proof of this bullshit, just something to show the courts, just something so that they've have no choice but to believe me. Then they'd see through her lies and see her for what she is. Like I say, I know that, strictly speaking, I shouldn't have done it, but I was desperate and frustrated. All that "Sarah's ill" business, the feeding Sarah lies about me... it was all too much.

I got out of the car and confronted her. "Why are you lying to the courts? Why are you trying to destroy the relationship between me and Sarah? Why are you abusing both of us?" Far from being terrified of this mad aggressive bastard – that's me – she launched into a barrage of swear words and abuse, accusing me of being all sorts of things. Little did she know, but I was taping the whole thing. That was another trick I picked up from the films. She made a complaint to the police that I was harassing her. The police upheld the charge and did me for harassment.

A couple of weeks later I did it again. Again she'd missed the contact and again I was angry. There was another thing. I'd been asking about Sarah's nursery. I didn't even know where she went to nursery and no one would tell me. I don't think it's too unreasonable for a father to know where his kid goes to nursery, do you? I don't think it's a crime. Actually, I'd call that a basic right. Oops, sorry. I forgot. I've got no rights. Sod that. I wanted to know.

I waited near the ex's mother's house, waited for Sarah to be dropped off as she always was. So again, I followed her to the nursery and just waited there. Watched the kids going in and waited. I did nothing else. I didn't want to do anything else. What else was I going to do? That was it. I just looked at Sarah from a distance, just watched her going into the nursery. It was heart-breaking but it was something I felt I had to do.

Maybe stupidly, I let her know that I now knew which nursery Sarah went to – big mistake. She made another complaint to the cops and said that – and I can quote here – that, "I threatened to slit her throat." It's such a stupid thing to say. If she'd have said that I threatened to take Sarah away or something, that would make more sense. But to say that I threatened to slit her throat, it was so stupid. Who on earth is going to believe that? Maybe she'd been watching the films as well – and gone for the really scary American ones. Whatever, the police believed it and charged me with harassment again. All those accusations that Jan had been making about my threats and aggression and stuff, it had done the trick. It had built up this picture, this image of me as being mad and out of control. This image of someone who would say something like "I'm going to slit your throat".

To charge someone with harassment, there has to be two incidents. And now they had their two incidents. It was like Jan and the cops were working together to stitch me up. You can say that I walked into it by following them and, maybe I did. But all I wanted to do was know what nursery my daughter was going to. Suddenly that's a crime. I don't know whether it's pathetic or funny.

On April 3rd I was arrested and charged with harassment. I was taken to the police station and down into the interview room and all I would say to them was "No comment", "No comment". After a while they said to me "Are you going to say anything apart from 'No comment'?" I said, "Yes, I'll say two things. One, she's an evil harassing child abuser and two, you lot are all bent." That went down well.

I thought I'd be OK at the harassment hearing. She was making all sorts of wild allegations about what I'd said and what I'd done and how I threatened her and all, but I had the ace. I'd taped it all. I had proof that I'd done nothing like that, that if anyone had used abusive language it was her. Imagine how I felt when Howlett Clarke and Cushman (this firm was already representing me on 'family' matters, and now also on this 'criminal' matter) told me that the tape was inadmissible in a court of law. I was the only one who had any proof. I was the only one who had any sort of evidence. And they were telling me that it was inadmissible? You can call me paranoid if you want, but really… wouldn't you be? I'm suing them for negligence now – you've got to see these things through. It's not that I feel, I don't know, responsible, but if you don't get these people they'll only do it again and some other poor bastard father will get stuffed. Same with Mahany and the 'inadmissible' psychiatrist report.

The magistrate just went along with police. Not surprising really. Well, it wasn't a surprise to me. Like I say, it's not that I was paranoid... I was charged. They said I had to have an electronic tag for three months. An electronic tag! What did they think I was? And I had a curfew not to leave my house between 8am and 1pm Monday to Friday because Sarah would be at nursery during that time. All I wanted to know was where Sarah went to nursery. I didn't want to stalk her. What did they think I wanted to do? If they'd have treated me like even half a human being and told me basic stuff like where my daughter went to nursery I wouldn't have to do anything like that. And can you imagine what they'd say if I didn't want to know what nursery she went to? They'd say I didn't care, that I was negligent.

But here I was. An electronic tag on my leg and a curfew not to leave my house during the week until 1pm. What? Not to get a loaf of bread? A newspaper? I was supposed to stay in all morning watching Richard and Judy? Why don't the courts concentrate on catching the real criminals rather than a dad who just wants to see his daughter?

Apart from anything to do with me and Sarah, they were denying me the ability to earn a living. I could have been a suicide bomber and I'd have been treated better than this. I really didn't understand it. I hadn't done anything and they knew I hadn't done anything. They knew I had the tape that proved my innocence and even if it was officially inadmissible in a court of law, they all still knew about it. Yet they were treating me like I was a big league criminal. Why? Also, and I've got to say this – even if I had done what they'd said, even if I had threatened Jan, did it really warrant a three month electronic curfew so that I couldn't leave the house? It was all beyond me.

I was ordered not to contact Jan directly or indirectly – like I ever wanted to talk to her again - and not to enter borough of Kingston-on-Thames, where Sarah's nursery was. I could only contact her through solicitor. I didn't want to contact her, directly or indirectly. I'd be happy if I never had to contact her, directly or indirectly, ever again. But we were linked together. Our lives would always be joined because of Sarah. Funny how something so beautiful and so pure can come out of something so shit.

This was a problem. It gave Jan an excuse not to come to the contact centres - and therefore Sarah wouldn't come either – because it was forbidden for us to meet.

In a letter from Howlett Clarke Cushman dated April 28th 2003: "Miss Green is not bringing Sarah to contact sessions because she states she is in fear for her safety. On the face of it, she should not breach the order which affords Sarah contact with you. Ultimately, if you are to have any contact at all with your daughter you will need to convince the court and Miss Green that there will not be any contact with Miss Green during before or after these sessions."

I know it's a simple idea and probably dumb, but... Why couldn't Jan's mother or anyone else bring Sarah?

You want to hear something really funny? I was going to tell you later, but now's as good a time as any. They were wrong. Howlett Clarke and Cushman were wrong. The tape would have been admissible. It should have been allowed. Where do I find these people? We'll deal with them later, I thought.

Just after the hearing I heard from Jan. Odds on I was going to. She wouldn't pass up an opportunity to have a bit of a gloat and wind me up. The real reason she hadn't been attending the contacts was, she said, that I was such a maniac that the police had advised her not to attend the contacts. I got her saying that on tape too. And I've got the police denying it on tape. And I've got my solicitors denying it. The police actually said that not only didn't they say that, but they were not allowed to say anything like that even if they privately believed it. All on tape. So Jan was done for wasting police time and harassing me. Actually... No she wasn't. She never is. No one ever says anything to mum.

It was all getting too much again. Everything seemed to be happening against me. Everything seemed to be getting out of control again. Every time I tried to do something, it went wrong. And every time she tried to do something it worked. And I wasn't doing anything wrong. Really, I wasn't doing anything wrong.

Back in December 2002, back in the good old days of Hamnett Osborne Tisshaw, I'd been told I'd have to get a psychiatrist, so I got a psychiatrist. They told me that Jan and I would share the costs. OK. Then they told me that I'd have to pay for it all myself. Again, OK. I didn't like it, but I did it. The psychiatrist was Dr Mary Lindsay. A nice enough woman, and I don't know how old she was, but she looked a bit past it. No disrespect but you've got to tell it like you see it.

She'd been taken on the previous December and had supposed to have had the report done by May 25th. Got it done? She hadn't even contacted my ex by that time. As Howlett Clarke Cushman said May 6th 2003: "Doctor Lindsay is having difficulty contacting Miss Green." Difficulty? By phone? Through her cleaning company? How hard could it be?

She's good, I thought. But then in a letter she said, "If and when I see your ex, I'm still going to be suggesting supervised contact". I thought about this. How could she say that if she's not even met her? How can she say that if she's not spoken to her? My ex could be a mix of Adolf Hitler and Fred West for all she knew. What's the point of us doing this if she's got such preconceived ideas? I was paying out £2,000 for this seemingly useless old biased doctor. It was completely obvious that she thought that as a father I was bad and Jan, as a mother, was good. I told Dr Lindsay on May 30th stop what you're doing now and send me back the rest of my money. That charade cost me £500.

It was time to start making more banners.

CHAPTER SIXTEEN

I thought about it a bit more this time. I tried to work out exactly what to do. I'd done two protests and they both hadn't been much good really. The first one was too high and no one knew I was there. The second one was in Guildford but – and no disrespect to Guildford – does anyone know where Guildford is? How many times do you see Guildford on the national news? No. If I was going to do another protest – and I was – it had to be right. It had to be somewhere where no one would miss it, where everyone would know all about it. I still wanted to be up high so that no one could get to me and it had to be really visible. London. I had to go back to London. I had wanted to be close to the House of Parliament but thee weren't any cranes nearby so Tower Bridge was the next best. High up, visible, famous. Tower Bridge. No one was going to miss that.

I had to do it quickly before that state sponsored curfew was imposed, so at 2am on June 15th 2003 I went up a 200ft crane by Tower Bridge. I decided that I wanted to something a bit more meaningful than simply go up and then come down. I wanted to say something, so I came up with this idea that I was going to stay up there for a significant amount of time. I decided on 62 hours – that was the amount of supervised contact Sarah and I had had since this whole business had begun. As it was I only stayed there until 11pm the following day. Why? Again I was conned.

I'd learnt from the protests I'd already done and really

took my time with this one. I made proper banners made out of old dust sheets and bed sheets. I took my time writing the words out first and then doing it properly with thick black gaffer tape.

I got up the crane easily enough. I was getting good at this lark by now. My best mate Pete came up with me and distracted the security guard. I settled myself at the top. It was hard work though. I had ten double sheets and a dust-sheet in one bag, and eight litres of water and some food in another. I had to put my arms through each handle with the bag pressed against my chest as I needed both hands for the ladder. God knows how much it weighed but it was so heavy it took me two trips to get it all up. Once up there, I got my banners out, put my stuff in the driver's cabin and waited.

After what seemed like no time at all a police negotiator was talking to me. They wanted to do a deal. This was impressive, this was what I'd been waiting for. The decision to do a protest in the centre of London by something as visible as Tower Bridge had obviously worked. If they wanted to talk so quickly, I must have been making an impression. I had a long chat with the police negotiator who seemed a really reasonable bloke. He said that if I came down now he'd write a letter to the courts stating that I was considerate and co-operative. He agreed that they wouldn't arrest me, that they would look into the case and study the evidence. He agreed that they would take my case to the family courts and examine it again.

I thought about it all, and realised that this was as good as I was going to get. I knew that they couldn't promise to give me my daughter back. I knew that they couldn't give me back our lost time. I knew that they couldn't just lock that ex of mine up just as they couldn't make her disappear. I agreed to come down. We set a time for 11pm. I also asked Taylor Woodrow, the construction company whose site and crane I had 'borrowed' to make a goodwill gesture – a donation – to Fathers 4 Justice, an organisation I'd talked to just before going up. Taylor Woodrow should have been happy. I had intended to disrupt their work for four or five days. As it was, I was only there one working day.

Fathers 4 Justice (F4J) has done well in raising people's awareness of this whole issue. It's only been going since 2002 and already membership has gone up from 200 to over 10,000, but a lot of it's gone bad. There are a few people at the top who are in it for themselves, for their own glory. There are some good people and, like I say, it's done some good, but I'm not a member. None of the protests I've done have been with Fathers 4 Justice. I operate by myself and, while I've got all the sympathy in the world for those guys and for all the other fathers in my situation, I can only act for myself. I hadn't co-ordinated with Fathers 4 Justice. I rang F4J and left a message on the day that I went up saying that I was going to do a protest that day, but none of my protests had anything to do with them and I hadn't met any of them by this time.

I agreed to come down at 11pm the following day. It bugged me a bit because I'd said to myself that I was going to be there for 62 hours and if I say something, generally I stick to it. But I'd given them my word and that was that. Also, after I'd said I was going to come down, and after I'd had a think about the 62 hours I started to change my mind about coming down. The copper said to me, "I thought you said you were a man of your word. You made an agreement with me, now you want to go back on it." He was right. I'd said I was going to come down, so I had to do it.

I'd taken the precaution of asking for a solicitor to be present during all that chat with the police negotiator. He was a new solicitor – not one of the 'monkeys' from Howlett. This was a bloke called Steve Holiday. I was naïve but not stupid. I didn't want to have a nice chat with them, come down and then find myself up against a wall with a pair of handcuffs on. He was a reasonable bloke and sorted it out and did make sure that I didn't get arrested.

"I did it for my daughter and all the other fathers betrayed by the legal system. Sarah's everything I live for. I want everyone to know of the injustice to forgotten fathers. The legal system is an institutionalised social scandal," I said to the reporters. The police were getting grief by the media about 'punishing' me, but a 'police spokesman' made a statement saying, "Police have no power of arrest as he was on private land. We will send a detailed report to site owner Taylor Woodrow for civil redress if they wish."

Taylor Woodrow said, "We're not going to prosecute. Mr Chick came down of his own accord. We felt he worked well with the police and the protest ended peacefully. We are comfortable with the conclusion."

I came down. I didn't get arrested, that was the good bit. The bad bit was that the police didn't do any of the things that they were supposed to do – no letters, no investigations, no back-up, nothing. And Taylor Woodrow didn't make any contribution. It wasn't a big deal – but you've got to think that their attitude wasn't great long-term thinking.

That Tower Bridge protest was a bit of an anti-climax for me. I'd put a lot of thought into it and a lot of work into it, but I'd let myself be distracted by the cops and, for some reason, I trusted them. Predictably my trust was betrayed but Tower Bridge wasn't all for nothing. Again, I learned how to do it properly and learning is good, isn't it. You never know when you might need that knowledge again.

When I came down I went to stay with a mate who'd driven down from Dagenham. He was in a similar position to me and had also been involved in protests for father's rights. Matt O'Connor from F4J was there too. Probably thought there'd be a photo opportunity. Matt had set himself up as the leader of F4J and was the sort of bloke who started off fine, but the media attention had gone to his head a bit. Once that started to happen, it seemed to become more important to him than anything else. Maybe that's being unfair to him, but that's the way it seems to me. I've got a bit of personal experience to back that up but we'll get round to all that. You've got to be very careful who you trust in this game. Suppose it's the same everywhere.

Steve Holiday agreed to take on my work and I dispensed with Howlett Clarke and Cushman. They'd not done anything for me, hadn't helped me at all. I changed to a firm of family solicitors called Barnes and Partners, from Edmonton in north London who'd been recommended to me by Holiday.

Outside of all this, something good had happened in my life. In early July 2003, I met Gemma. She's an absolute diamond, but I'm not going to talk about her so much because that invades her privacy. It's my decision to write about my life here and it wouldn't be fair if I plastered her life all over its pages. I just want to say one thing: I really think if it hadn't been for Gemma I would have lost it. She's everything that my ex isn't. She's honest and warm and supportive and loving and truthful and beautiful. The stress that this whole business has caused us... you wouldn't believe. Sometimes – probably more than sometimes – I haven't been the easiest bloke to be with. My work has suffered. My income has been shot. My life has, in many ways, been wrecked by this whole business. But she's stood by me, supported me. And it's jumping ahead of the game a bit, but she's fantastic with Sarah.

*　*　*　*

You might be thinking now, "What's happened to the contacts? Is he going to the centres? How's Sarah getting on?" I guess you're thinking that about now because back then when I was living through all this bullshit that what I was thinking too.

Basically, the answers to those questions are "Nothing", "No" and "I wish I knew". I'd been reborn, re-branded as a man with a tag on his leg who goes around harassing people. That's the way the police saw me, anyway. Me, I was just frustrated because all I wanted to do was what I'd wanted to do from day one: see my little girl. But I wasn't allowed to. I'd also have liked to be able to get a job but I couldn't do that either because of the curfew. When most people go to work I was stuck at home, not allowed out of the house. As for how Sarah was getting on... that question was doing my head in.

The ex had been trying to get me to crack, trying to get me to break. Trying to show the world that I was this mad, aggressive, violent idiot and I don't know how I didn't turn into that person. The frustration inside me was that great. It was like a volcano, ready to burst. I had nothing to do, nowhere to go, nowhere to put my energy, nothing to do with my time... it was all doing my head in.

On June 12th, I received a letter from David Irwin, the Cafcass Children and Family Reporter. "I have been asked by Guildford County Court to prepare a report to help reach a decision about future arrangements for Sarah. I would like to propose a meeting with you at this office..." And where was "this office"? Richmond Road, Kingston. And where was I banned from? Kingston. It was nice to know that this Cafcass officer had his finger on the pulse and knew so much about us.

A month later, after he'd seen us both – separately, of course – we received a letter from him relating to his report. They're funny things, these reports. On first glance, they look fine. But the more you look at it, the more it seems that the phrases relating to her are a whole lot more friendly than the phrases relating to me. It's all, "Ms Green said...", Ms Green tells me...", "Ms Green agrees that...", "She says...", "Her view..." and "Mr Chick considers...", "Mr Chick is extremely angry...", "Mr Chick might have..." and "Mr Chick's solicitor... ". It's only a small thing, but the inference is clearly that Mr Chick is the hostile one.

In fairness, he did say that Mrs Macaulay at Woking Contact Centre "had said that the actual contact between

Sarah and her father was excellent". Jan wrote a letter to Mrs Macaulay complaining on September 15th. "I am very concerned as to how you have come to this conclusion." Well Jan, because she's the one who actually sees us together, that's how. But anyway, shouldn't you be pleased that your daughter gets on well with her father? It's you who doesn't get on with me, not her.

Jan tried to infer that during the contacts during the early part of 2003, Sarah had been crying and upset. It's true. She had. It's also true that Mrs Macaulay reported on February 17th, 2003: "Contact with David and his daughter has been good. There has been the odd occasion when Sarah has been tired or not well and she has cried but David has managed to calm her without any help… Again, I state that contact is very good."

David Irwin noted Jan's complaint and wrote back on September 24th, 2003: "I am told that Mr Chick did nothing wrong and was attentive to advice given by staff. This news that Sarah was happy during the contacts in 2002 but upset during the early contacts of 2003 does beg the question as to why Sarah behaved in such a different manner to that of the previous successful session of December 21st, 2002." It did indeed beg the question, but as far as Mr Irwin was concerned, begging the question was sufficient. You didn't have to actually ask – or investigate – that question. Leave it open-ended. Let people's imaginations take them where you want them to go but you can't say it. And you can't say it because there's no proof. No evidence. No basis of fact.

They're onto you, I thought. It's not too hard to answer that begged question. The answer is this: It's not too hard to make a child upset if you want to. Don't let her get enough sleep. It's easy. The real question that should be begged was a different one: What sort of person would deliberately make a child upset just so they could make a father look bad?

On October 10th, my solicitors Barnes and Partners wrote to Jan: "You have unilaterally ceased bringing Sarah to the centre notwithstanding that there has been no order of the court terminating contact. In the circumstances we must insist that contact at the very least resume as ordered by the court. We therefore request you contact us…"

"We therefore request" never did make much difference in this business, and needless to say it didn't this time either. I sat in my house, thinking and planning and plotting. That last crane protest had been short but it had been the best one so far. In terms of how I went about it and how it was seen, it was the most effective one. It was good but it was cut short. I let the police get in my head. What I had to do, I decided, was do it again but even more properly. It was an inevitable decision. After all that sitting at home – all tagged up and nowhere to go – I had to do something.

I decided to do Tower Bridge again. It was a perfect place to do that sort of thing – and also I fancied doing it there to piss Taylor Woodrow off because they'd gone back on the deal they did with me to make a donation to F4J. My curfew ended on October 30th and the day after that I went. Well, why wait? When you've made your mind up to do something, why wait?

I'd been talking to friends and mates from F4J about tactics and things. Trying to work out the best way to go about it. This was when the whole dressing up as superheroes thing started. When we were talking we realised that to every kid their father is a superhero. Regardless of what the State and organisations like Cafcass said, regardless of how we were seen by anyone else, to the kids – and these were the only people we were really concerned about – to the kids, their dads were superheroes. So why not present ourselves like that?

It was, we thought, the perfect protest. We knew we had to do something that was peaceful, something that couldn't be described as violent or twisted into being seen as violent by the media. The reason we were in this position in the first place was that we'd been labelled as violent or aggressive or something like that. It was important that we didn't give anyone any excuse to say, "You see, I told you so". Like Bob Geldof said, "Of all the possible responses, laughing with scorn in the face of injustice is one of the best. And infinitely preferable to violence." Right.

If we dressed up as superheroes it would get the point across all right. It would make people smile and get their attention. It would make us a little bit more visible. A bloke doing a protest is one thing. A bloke dressing up as a superhero doing a protest is something else. The more we thought about it, the more we thought that that's the route we were going to go down.

This was the first time I'd thought about doing something like this with someone else. I don't mean doing it with them, I just mean talking about it and planning it and that. Before, I was isolated, just doing my own thing. Even now I was on my own really. Matt O'Connor, had said that he wanted nothing happening at the moment, and when he got wind of my plan to do another Tower Bridge protest he said that he didn't want me to do it. But I had had enough of waiting, of sitting around. Inaction had got me nowhere. Basically I do what I do. What other people think... that's up to them. To be honest, when Matt said he didn't want me to do it then, I don't think it had anything to any great idea or plan or any strategy he had. I think he just didn't want someone coming along and getting more publicity than him. F4J is a good organisation, lots of good people there, but there's a few people at the top who use it to further themselves, you know? If they stay in charge, it makes them look like the big man, makes them look like the important ones.

A couple of weeks or so before I went up the crane again, another bloke from Father's 4 Justice went up the Royal Courts Of Justice dressed as Batman. It got a little press coverage, and I thought it was cool. And when I saw it, I finally decided that's what I was going to do. I was going to become that superhero.

The next question is "Why Spiderman?" Well, the first thing I've got to say is that it was nothing to do with Spiderman being Sarah's favourite hero. I never ever said that. It was just something that someone wrote in a newspaper. It's a good line and it conjures up a nice picture, but it isn't true. That's really something I've noticed since this I started doing my protests. The papers can say what they like and no one cares. I know people, celebrities and that, always say that but it's only when you're in that situation yourself that you really notice what's happening. Like that thing about Spiderman being Sarah's favourite superhero. Someone just made it up. It's stupid really.

Basically, I didn't want do to Batman because it had been done, so I went to the fancy dress shop and the two costumes they had were Spiderman and Superman, and not being big-headed, I didn't want to be Superman. Maybe I should have. Anyway, Spiderman's cool I think and, as an image it made sense for me to take that one. I was the bloke who climbed up the tall structures, just like Spiderman. I was the one who hung around way up high. For what I was doing, for the type of protest I was getting known for, Spiderman was the perfect image. I liked the idea of climbing a crane by Tower Bridge as Spiderman. If this thing was going to get any media attention, if it was going to get noticed, that would be a picture. It would have been different if I was doing something down on the ground or something, but... no. Spiderman. It suited me.

I knew this one was going to be more serious and my preparations for it were as thorough as always. I went to London to see which cranes were doing what. And there weren't that many cranes at the right angle, so there weren't that many others that were suitable. It's probably not something you think about in normal life, the angle of the cranes. But if you want to go climbing onto one, you've got to think about these things. The arm of the crane can't be pointing up or else you're going to have trouble climbing out onto the arm to put your banners up. And it can't be pointed down because of the same thing. If it's pointed down, it's going to be dangerous. It's got to be just right.

I looked round the same site as I did last time again. Whatever they were building, they were taking their time. I wanted to do the same site because I still felt a bit angry about being stitched up by them last time. While I was doing the last protest, all the people on the site like the Taylor Woodrow people they were all saying, "Yeah, come down". I co-operated with them, and they said I was considerate and that they would contribute to my cause, but as soon as I was down, they didn't and I thought that was a bit naughty.

There were three cranes on the site. I did the highest one the first time, but this time round I noticed that the security was much tighter now – can't imagine why that would have been – and so I went for the crane nearest the edge of the site because it was the easiest one to get on to. I took up all the usual things – a bit of food like biscuits and sausage rolls, fags, toilet paper, crowbar, phone, walkie-talkie, clothes, toothbrush and paste and about six to eight litres of water. And it was pissing down so I had to take up some plastic sheeting. It was a big struggle taking that lot up but if you want to stand up and be counted, you have to do it regardless of the weather.

I had a big holdall crammed with banners and the water all tied up nice and small, but it was such hard work getting up there. It wasn't only the weight of the bags though that was bad enough. It was the size of the space by the ladder. The ladder that went up was one of those that had bars going round the back as a safety feature, and it might have made it safer if you slipped, but it wasn't designed for blokes carrying big hold-alls. I had to trail the bags up by my side while still using one hand to hold on and climb. It wasn't the easiest thing I've ever done.

I didn't put on the Spiderman outfit on until I was up there. I thought about it beforehand and I've got to admit I would have felt a bit of an idiot climbing up that ladder dressed up as Spiderman. Although the image kind of made me smile. Even so, I did feel a little bit of a twat when I put it on when I was up there. You know what fancy dress costumes are like. Even if you're just going to a party dressed up you feel a twat. This was like that, but a hundred times more. But I didn't care. I did it to raise public awareness of what's going on, and the reporting about it and the decision to go up as Spiderman caused a lot more coverage than if I'd just gone up as myself.

Despite everything I've done, I'm not the sort of bloke who likes being the centre of attention. I don't normally like people looking at me, but you've got to do what you've got to do and if you're going to stand on a crane in the centre of London dressed up as a comic book superhero... you might as well get used to people looking at you.

It's funny in a sense. It was only when I put on a fancy dress costume and started walking around as Spiderman that people took the whole thing seriously and what I was doing became part of a serious movement. When I was just an ordinary looking desperate dad, no one took any notice. I don't know what that's about, but it does make you think a bit. You've got to dress up like a twat to make people take you seriously. That says something.

*   *   *   *

I went up Thursday night/Friday morning at about 2am, and settled myself down. Sorted myself out. Put my things away and got my banners out.

The banners I had were more professional this time too. There was a professional F4J banner – "In The Name Of The Children". The other big banner I had read "(*Real name of ex*) The She Devil Cleaning Co Chessington And Incompetent Judge Critchlow Reading/Guildford Stop Abusing My Child and I". It's strange but no one said anything about that. I'd just been up on a harassment charge – Not Guilty, but there you go. Yet here I was, telling the world what I thought of Jan and Judge Critchlow and no one said anything. No slander. No harassment. Nothing. There was nothing said about defamation of character or contempt. Nothing. I had another six or seven banners up with me, all with various declarations about bias and discrimination.

There was quite a small driver's cabin up there, but it was okay for what I needed. I was only getting about two to three hours of sleep up there, and it was enough for me and my stuff. I had a few empty water bottles up there for pissing - the crane driver probably pisses in a cup too – and a few plastic carrier bags to shit in. (Those bags I left on top of the crane despite what the police reported. They said that I'd thrown my poo at them, but they should know that my poo is too good for them. I wouldn't do that. I was up there for a serious cause and I wasn't playing or messing. Maybe they would have treated people like that, but I wouldn't. But, and here's something freaky, there's police photos of my shit in plastic bags. Really. They took photos of all that. I don't know what that's all about.)

Immediately it was obvious that this protest was different from the other ones. I'd only been up there a few hours when the first people started noticing me up there. That was at 5am, and that's when the police turned up and before long they'd closed one side of Tower Bridge. The arm of the crane that I went up was hanging right out across Tower Bridge. So when they shut one side of the bridge, I went out the rest of the way to the end of the arm. So then they shut both sides of the bridge. I don't know why they reacted like this, as all previous protests had all been a bit of a damp firework.

But whatever. That's the reason I think why it all went so well so quickly. As soon as the police took the decision – actually I found out later that it wasn't so much a decision as a tactic - to shut Tower Bridge, the scale of the whole protest escalated. The statement they put out said,

"Originally we calculated all the potential things that could happen, including the man throwing missiles into the road or jumping from the crane. We had a duty of care to the public, however much congestion it caused. If he decided to jump or throw a lump of concrete on to a car with four kids inside, what would people say about the police then?"

The road closures were what got all the news. In a sense I didn't mind because although it detracted from what I was protesting about because most of the press coverage was about road closures, it made people notice what I was doing. Whenever they wrote about the road closures and what a pain in the arse I was, they had to write something like "David Chick, who's protesting about... " and that was enough. That made people think about what I was doing and why I was doing it.

The other reason the protest went so well was that I was quite determined that I wasn't going to be talked down by any police negotiator – real or otherwise – like I had been in the past. I was going to stay up there as long as I had to stay up there and for once I stuck to that. I'd been up cranes three times before and whereas before I let the police get in my head, this time I didn't. I'd had enough of their policies, of their tricks and their little games. The more I thought about it, the more determined I was. All that stuff how I'd been abused by the system, how they were trying to destroy the relationship between me and my daughter was going round my head and the more I thought about it, the harder it made me concentrate on the job in hand.

The story was broadcast all round the world. I was aware of how much was on because I had a walkie-talkie and a radio, and I listened to Capital Radio and heard everything they were saying about me. I listened to the phone-ins and I listened to top policemen and people like the Mayor slagging me off. There are words I could use...

It was the road closures that made Spiderman impossible to avoid. It was the road closures that caused all the fuss.

The Times newspaper reported that the tailbacks on the roads went back 10 miles and that I'd cost business £50m. The Federation of Small Businesses said the cost of my actions was "£10m a day." Taylor Woodrow said that the protest was stopping 120 builders from working on their £45million office development.

The police tried to pin it all on me. They wanted to get the public to see me as a nuisance, as selfish, as the idiot who'd caused all this. If their figures are to be believed, it was all a very expensive public relations exercise. Richard Walford, the Chief Inspector, went out and said: "We don't want to close the roads; we apologise for any inconvenience caused to the business community and residents of London. As soon as we can possibly open the roads we will do so. This is out of our hands, it's in the hands of the demonstrator. He knows what he is doing, he knows what his actions are and he knows that as soon as he safely comes down from the crane we will then open the cordon."

I knew that they were playing a psychological game with me. There was no need to close those roads. They knew from my previous protest that I wasn't going to jump off. What on earth would I do that for? Killing myself would do wonders for my relationship with Sarah, don't you think? I don't throw things. I never have. I don't do things like that. I do a peaceful protest. They all knew that. It wasn't like it was the first time I'd done anything like this. But while I knew all that, it was hugely frustrating. They were putting out all the lies and even if I knew that eventually it would all come out, right now it was frustrating. When someone pumps out a load of rubbish about you and you can't say or do anything about it... I wanted them to all be talking about the *issues*, the reasons I was up there, but all they are interested in is the excitement of whether I'm a madman, or a suicide jumper or some overgrown kid having a tantrum at a hundred feet up or something. **What about social injustices?** I wanted to scream at them. Report the news. Talk about issues. Call for social change.

It was all rubbish, the crane had been operational over the roads for months and nothing had happened. No one had died, you know. Cranes hang over roads all over the place and nothing happens. Anyway, I sent down a message saying that they could send a crane driver up to twist the crane round so it didn't overhang the road. I was quite happy to have someone come up and do that. But they wouldn't do it. Why? Because they thought I'd hold him hostage? That I'd throw him over the side? No, they wouldn't do it because if they did, that would be the end of their propaganda against me.

What I was saying was basically that the law was wrong and that it needed changing. It doesn't matter how justified you are, it doesn't matter how wrong the law is. But the thing is, the police are never going to stand there and say "Yeah, you're right. The law is wrong", so if they're going to be right, they've got to make the public believe that you're wrong. Simple as that.

I issued a statement which I hoped would put the attention back where it should be.

"I was there at my daughter's birth. I fed her, I bathed her, I played with her for the first 10 months. Then my ex partner suddenly wiped her out my life and there is nothing I can do about it and the courts assist it all. It is an absolute scandal.

"The corrupt family law needs exposing for more and more children are losing their fathers and some of these fathers top themselves or kill their former partners and sometimes kill their kids.

"It could all be changed so easily but who cares about fathers and children? My ex thinks she is going to provoke me into going round and losing my rag and doing something bad to her which I have never done. I have got to the end of my tether - this is my cry for help.

"It's too late for me to be able to assist my relationship with my daughter. It's already destroyed but hopefully my protest will assist the fathers and children of tomorrow."

Then I added a message to Sarah: *"I love you darling. I hope to see you soon. I am missing you like mad."*

*   *   *   *

Once the publicity started, once Spiderman started to get a bit of media attention, everyone tried to get in on the act. The Mayor of London, Ken Livingstone, someone who's always had an eye on the front pages – looking to see if his picture was on them? - said, "I've spoken to Metropolitan Police Commissioner Sir John Stevens about the situation and we both agree it was completely unacceptable.

"Action has to be taken to allow Londoners to move around the city and not be held to ransom by one individual. He is a man who is putting his own life at risk, police officers at risk, other Londoners who may be passing along the road at risk. He is causing a huge inconvenience to Londoners and is not necessarily the role model one wants for one's children as they grow up - particularly since he also dresses in funny clothes.

"If anyone wanted to demonstrate that some men should not have access to their own children at their own will and whim, Mr Chick is amply demonstrating why women don't always feel they want their partners to have access to their children. The idea that an individual can hold London to ransom is completely unacceptable. We would not put up with it if it was Osama bin Laden. I do not see why anyone would expect we would put up with it for this man. I believe Bin Laden and Saddam are helpless with laughter at the way London has been brought to a standstill by a comic book hero."

What a twat. Did he really say *"Why some men should not have access to their own children at their own will and whim?"* What? That was a dangerous thing to say. Clearly the words of someone who didn't know what they were talking about. And all that stuff about funny clothes and bin Laden and that, it was just a cheap try to get a laugh, but I think the public is smarter than that. I think people realised that a bloke didn't do what I was doing if it wasn't really important. Later that year there was a Personality Of The Year award vote in the London Evening Standard and guess where Livingstone came – and guess where I came. I was second and he was about tenth or something. That shows you what happens when the public gets a chance to speak.

Actually Ken Livingstone's just a muppet who did what he was told by the police. I've got copies of incident logs where the police tell him what they want him to say. It was their tactics to close all the roads, and it was their attempt to turn the public against me, and Livingstone was being told what to say by the police, but we'll get onto that.

The deputy chairman of the Metropolitan Police Authority, Richard Barnes, said the extra policing cost of the protest was £10,000 a day. "I would like David Chick to receive a bill afterwards. If we can charge David Blaine, let us charge him as well. Although I understand why Mr Chick was protesting, it does not give him the right to be an absolute prat." (David Blaine was an American magician who'd sat in a see through box for a month suspended above the Thames. He was a publicity seeking twat whereas I was trying to make a legitimate peaceful political protest about social injustice. About flaws in a flawed system that allows fathers to sink to the bottom and become invisible.)

Not everyone was hostile. The former Conservative minister David Mellor – the one who got sacked because his mistress sold a story to the tabloids about how he liked to dress up as a Chelsea footballer when they had sex - said "It's ludicrous. Thousands of people are being inconvenienced because the police lack any common sense and there isn't a politician who can tell them what to do. If you have a burglary in your street you won't see a policeman. Why? Because they are dealing with a 'serious incident' on a crane in St. Katharine's Dock."

The papers got hold of a mate, who said: "He is a desperate man. He is strong-minded and you have to be to go through this disgusting court system. What we are all fighting for is the legal presumption of equal responsibility for parenting. He's a tough old boy. It was pelting down with rain and it was really slippery when he climbed up. David and I have shared a few tears in the past and he was very emotional just as he went up. He doesn't really like heights but he is a desperate man. I watched him from my vehicle and I just don't know how he found the strength to go up there. He had to get through the building site and use a scaffold pole to get up to the main structure of the crane, which was completely wet. It was freezing cold last night and teeming down with rain - very slippy up there and very dangerous. But like any man he will do anything to see his children."

The story got covered all over the world, in The Straights Times in Asia, The Alternative News Network in Queensland, Australia, The Salt Lake Tribune in America and other newspapers and TV and radio stations in the UK, the USA, New Zealand, Canada, Australia, India, South Africa and Singapore. More than I ever thought about, but would it get me closer to what I wanted? We'll see.

Matt O'Connor must have had mixed feelings about all this. On the one hand, the cause he supported was getting loads of publicity, and that was good for the cause and it also meant that he had loads of people sticking microphones in his face and he loves all that. But on the other hand, it was all because of me, all he was talking about was me – and that wasn't his favourite subject.

He started off supporting me, and said: "In the extra 20 minutes you spend in traffic think about this - one child will lose contact with their father in that time. At the end of today a further 100 kids will lose contact with their fathers. Do you really think a man is going to climb a crane over Tower Bridge for the fun of it in wet, windy and near freezing conditions for several days? Or is he doing it for the love of his daughter who he hasn't seen in eight months? We are at a loss as to why surrounding roads have been closed. This man is not suicidal and poses no threat to the public."

But when all the negative press started and he thought that the public were turning against me, he changed horses. "We can't control every angry dad who had been denied access to their children. We have got a massive problem here and it needs to be addressed by the government. It has taken guts to go up there and do that. You can label him a madman; I just label him a father who loves his daughter. We would not have done this ourselves but it has raised the level of debate about whether or not it is right that we create a nation of children growing up without fathers."

And, later, when I decided to come down... he tried to grab the glory: "We're pleased we helped to bring the protest to an end. We worked with the police and got him to agree not to go on the arm of the crane, meaning roads could be re-opened."

At the end, Metropolitan Police Commissioner Sir John Stevens said: "I'm perfectly happy with the operation. Once I'd decided that the conditions had changed we re-opened the roads. We have to take note of the health and safety issues for the public and the police and it was a successful operation. But we will review it. Everyone is very concerned about congestion for Londoners and anything we can do to minimise that we will do."

CHAPTER SEVENTEEN

There isn't a feeling like it. Standing on top of the world with everyone looking at you. Okay, so I still felt a bit of a twat being dressed up but even so, if I'm honest there was a part of me that enjoyed the attention. I was on my own up there. I was in control. And there'd been so much that had happened that was outside my control – from the way Jan had treated me to the way Cafcass had disrespected me to the way the system had abused me. And don't forget I'm a bloke who was forced to wear an electronic tag for three months... For me to be in control of a situation was a fantastic feeling.

I went up on the Friday and on the Saturday there were quite a lot of people there. I had a bit of support from F4J and there was all the publicity from the road closures and that, and it all combined to get a lot of people along to see this bloke dressed up as Spiderman hanging off this crane. If I hadn't been him, I'd have been curious to see what it was all about.

I could see groups of kids walking around down below and they were waving at me and I was waving back and they were shouting up "Spiderman!" That was good because I wanted to get the kids attention, and I wanted to give them a bit of a smile. Obviously it's all about kids what we're doing, and if they see you like that it makes them think about it a little bit. It makes them laugh which is always good, and it makes them think. They see me like that and they'll ask why is there a bloke doing that. They're not going to read a paper or sit and watch the news, are they?

Saturday was quite, I don't know, it was exciting what with everything going on. It seemed that maybe we could make some progress. But Sunday was different. It was quite deserted and the weather wasn't too clever. That was the day it really did drag. There was no-one down below and I was quite isolated and I had the police saying to me "Look Dave, all your supporters have gone now. You've done well, come along now." But I knew that all the time the roads were closed it was making the story bigger and bigger. The last two protests I'd done I'd let the police get inside my head and con me down and I wasn't going to let them get to me no more. I was going to stick it out.

By the fifth day the media attention was at its height. I knew I'd become a big news story because of all the people hanging around down on the ground and stuff, and I had my mobile, a radio and the walkie-talkie, but I think the moment it really sunk in was when I looked up and saw a Sky News helicopter buzzing around. It really was a massive media scrum down below.

The police were still pumping out all the publicity and they still had the roads closed, insisting I was a danger. The longer it went on, they thought, the more people would get pissed off with the inconvenience and the more they'd turn against Spiderman. They wanted people to just see me as a nuisance. But it didn't work. They also thought that I'd give up and cave in. After all, I'd done that before, I'd come down before I'd said I would so why wouldn't I this time? What they were figuring was that I'd come down, they could pin all the road closures on me and that would be that. But I wasn't coming down. I held out.

They were treating me the same way they treat terrorists and people like that. And all I am is a bloke who wants to see his daughter. How did things get to this stage? Back in December 2000 when Sarah was born I was the happiest bloke in the world. It was like someone had just opened the windows and let the sunlight in. It was like suddenly it was daytime and not night, you know what I mean? How did it go from that to me standing on top of a crane by Tower Bridge dressed up as Spiderman taking a dump in a plastic bag and trying to dodge a Sky News helicopter? How the fuck did that happen? I'd call it a nightmare but the word doesn't come close.

Then, after four days of giving everyone all this road, health and safety bullshit... suddenly everything changed and they opened all the roads up again. What had changed? I hadn't gone away. Maybe Government quickly passed a law to change all the health and safety requirements. More like they just change things around to suit their own purposes. That's the trouble with these people. They've got no principles.

I know why they decided to open the roads when they did. I'd had a chat with Matt O'Connor on the walkie-talkie at about 5pm on the Wednesday, and I was thinking then of coming down. I'd seen it all and I'd achieved what I'd wanted to achieve. I'd got more publicity for my case than I thought possible and I'd got a load of publicity for the cause and for Fathers 4 Justice. Also, I was getting a bit low on cigarettes, food and water. I said to Matt that I'd done it, that as far as I was concerned I could end it in an hour or two. He said, "No, don't. Wait till the morning." But – and I didn't know this at the time - the police heard me. They were listening to me on the walkie talkie all the time. So when they got wind of the idea that I was going to come down they took the decision to open the roads.

If they open the roads and then I come down, they'll claim that I only came down because they opened the roads. That way it becomes seen as their decision to open the roads that ended this protest. It was like they wanted to look good. Do you get it? If they do that it's like them saying "We're not going to be held to ransom but this guy any more. We're going to get on with our lives and London will not stop". Then I come down and they're all, "We won."

They put out a statement: "Whilst disruption to traffic in that area and the ability of Londoners to go about their day-to-day business unhindered are important factors, the health and safety of the public and our officers are of over riding concern. We are satisfied at the current time that all considerations have been taken into account and it is safe for the MPS to reopen these roads."

I had been thinking about staying up there for the night of November 5th. Not wanting to make it sound like I was having a laugh or anything, but it would have been fantastic to see all the fireworks over London from up top there. It would have been a fantastic sight. Mind you, I could have been hit by a rocket I suppose, but no, I wanted to see the fireworks. I did actually have some up there, and I let them off on the Wednesday. It was purple smoke, the colours of equality, but actually from where I was it was a bit grey and pathetic.

I came down on that Wednesday at 4pm and was arrested at the bottom of the crane as soon as I came down. I knew that was going to happen though. There was a load of press and that filming Spiderman coming down and so the police aren't going to stand around and shake my hand as I come down, are they? "Well done son. Fancy a beer?" They're not going to do that, are they? They've got to be seen to be dealing with me like a criminal, treating me tough. It's all that "And let this be a lesson to the rest of you" bollocks.

There was a few press and that but not a particularly big F4J group which was a bit disappointing. I thought they might make more of a show, but I guess they had their reasons. Also, it would have been useful in terms of publicity but in a way it was fair enough. I knew people would see me and immediately think that I was one of them, but I'd made it quite clear that I was nothing to do with them and they were nothing to do with me. I was just acting on my own and anything they did was riding on my story.

I was whipped into the police van while I was still in costume – that never happened to Spiderman, did it? – and the police took me to the station, Lime House I think it was. I was interviewed that same night and then kept in overnight. The next morning I appeared in court. I had the clothes I went up in and I'd changed back into those. I'd love to say that I was still in the Spiderman costume because that would have been fantastic, standing there in court in full Spiderman costume and showing the whole thing up for the farce that it was. But on the other hand I didn't want them to see it as a joke, I wanted them to take it as seriously as I was taking it.

This was my life. This was what I had been forced to become. I was an ordinary bloke living an ordinary life and being really quite happy with it. They had turned me into this publicity-seeking geezer who spent his whole life either up a crane or in a courtroom. This wasn't what I wanted, and… Sorry, but when was the last time I saw Sarah?

I was charged with causing a public nuisance. Stupid phrase. A nuisance. To put this into perspective, let me tell you something far worse than a nuisance. Having state-endorsed child-theft, that's worse. It's heart-breaking.

The court was a farce too. There was a black prosecutor and she was saying to the judge that I was "causing a destruction to all the neighbours nearby". She was supposed to be saying "disruption". She couldn't even talk properly. She was going, "Mr Chick was causing destruction…" We were in the court and the police couldn't even organise a prosecutor who could fucking tell the difference between disruption and destruction. The whole court, which was packed, was cracking up.

I got bail. When you get police bail what happens is that you're allowed to go out but you can only go out under certain conditions and you have to go back to court at a later date for the actual trial. Bail basically means that you're okay because the alternative to that is being kept in prison until the trial. The application for bail is made for you by your solicitor or barrister and normally it's a formality. But this time when they did that the police tried to oppose it. They don't like people like me, they don't like people who oppose police authority. They use whatever authority they've got to suppress us, and they knew that it would have been quite a head fuck to keep me in prison for four or five months until the trial. And that's what they wanted to do. But they failed. For once, my barrister or my solicitor did enough. I was bailed with certain conditions: to live and sleep each night at my home address, not to climb any tall structures, buildings or otherwise, and not to display myself in a fashion which is likely to cause destruction, sorry, I mean disruption. Basically, I could go home as long as I promised not to do it again. The District Judge Jacqueline Comyns said in summing up, "It's very simple what that means, Mr Chick: no more protests and no more standing up on cranes."

When I got home I found that while I was up the crane the police had been round and they'd taken my computer. Apparently they said it was to check if I was a paedophile. Fuck off. What I am is a dad. It was months before I got my computer back. They tried to do me for being public nuisance, for inconveniencing people but that's what they did to me. I was doing a peaceful protest and I was being abused and inconvenienced. That's why I got a "Not Guilty" verdict because the jury heard all the evidence and it wasn't hard to see that basically it was all police bullshit, bullshit, bullshit and I think generally juries do see through that, don't they?

After that everything calmed down again. There was a bit of media attention, the odd phone call from things like Bella magazine and people like that. A feller from a press agency in London would get on to me occasionally, and a lot of them said that they'd keep my number and get back in touch, but they didn't.

*   *   *   *

There's one question that everyone asked. One thing that everyone wanted to know. The question – and it's probably one that's occurred to you more than once – was this: Who's this ex? Who is Jan and what does she say?

All the papers were, naturally, going to my ex to get her side of the story. I've got documents proving that she was offered £18,000 by The Sun for her side of the story, for her to basically say why she didn't want me to see my daughter and why she thought I was a bad father. And she didn't answer. She wouldn't do an interview. Why wouldn't she do an interview? She'd made all these claims to the courts and the hearings about how skint she was, about how she didn't have any money. Well, here was a chance for her to grab a quick 18 grand and she turned it down. It doesn't add up, does it?

I'd have thought she would have done it to get her side of the story out. She said that she didn't do it on moral reasons, that she didn't want Sarah reading about it all in the future. It sounds very noble doesn't it? Well, it would do if it wasn't total bollocks. I know why she didn't do it. If she starting talking to a newspaper and saying to a paper all the things that she'd been saying in the family courts, she'd have been found out for the pathetic liar that she is. In the family courts she could say anything and because they're all held behind closed doors, in secret like, no one ever found out. But if she went public with those lies… that would be it: game over. I have evidence to disprove at least 90% of what she says.

She knew I wasn't a bad father and she knew there was no decent reason why I shouldn't be seeing Sarah. Anything that she would say, she'd just show herself up to be everything I was saying she was. The other thing she knew is that if she lied in print, I'd sue her, and then it really would be "Goodnight, Jan".

She did say two things while I was up the crane. She said, "Has he fallen off yet?" and "If I told you what I thought of him it would all be swear words." How stupid is she? I mean, could she have said anything that would have made her look more stupid if she'd tried? It made her look stupid and cold, and it made her look nasty. Not the sort of words you'd say about a good mother. Or is it just me who thinks that? Don't know. Don't care either. But even then, why make two stupid comments like that? Why not take the £18 grand and use it for Sarah, for Sarah's education. She's meant to be like seriously in debt, but she knows she can't do it because at the end of the day, if she said anything I can disprove anything she says. So she couldn't do it. Simple as that. So she's reduced to making stupid comments.

Funnily, The Sun only went to her because they didn't get me. When I was up the crane, there were some reporters from The Sun and they held up a poster saying that they wanted my story and there was a number for me to call them on. The Sun wanted the police to tell me that they wanted my story, but the cops wouldn't do that. They said that it would encourage other people to do the same thing as I was doing. The Sun wanted my story, but they then went to her. They didn't care about the truth, they just wanted a story.

After that, I did an exclusive interview with The Daily Mail and got a few quid for that – nothing like the 18 grand she was offered, but then again that fits. This whole story is how the mothers get more than the fathers. As a piece, the thing in The Mail was okay. It didn't really stick to why I did it. There's so much that's gone on over the past three years, the stories about how me and my daughter have been had over by the system, all the things that Cafcass have done and all the things my ex has done. Then there's the police involvement, the protest... There was too much to get in a newspaper article and while it was alright, it could have been done better.

I gave a few thousand quid out of The Daily Mail money to Fathers 4 Justice because it was a cause I believed in – well, it's the same cause as I was fighting for. There were a few dodgy characters there, people who might not be entirely straight, people who might not be there for the good of the cause, but there's dodgy characters everywhere. I was skint, but I thought it was a good thing to do at the time. Now, I regret giving them that money. While I was up the crane and that, they milked me for everything: they got loads of publicity out of it, and they got some money. Since then though, I got nothing from them. No help. No support, nothing.

But I did have a bit of a situation with them - or rather, a bit of a situation with Matt O'Connor. He said to me before I went up the crane that he didn't want me to do it, but he knew he couldn't control me. Then when I went up there, he was straight over there doing the big man thing and milking it for all he could, going on Sky and all the news channels and that. As soon as it was over, like I said, I donated them thousands of pounds and I don't know what happened to that. Maybe it went straight into his pocket? Or maybe he poured is straight down his throat? I don't know. Whatever. I got no support or nothing from him. Why? Because I did that protest and it went so well, I think he was a bit envious of me getting some of his glory because he wants all the credit for when the law is changed. That's what Matt's game is. He seems to wants the glory and the fame. He wants to get all the credit for what everyone does. But to me it's not about that. To me, it's about getting the law changed, it doesn't matter how you do it.

I did have a bit of grief with the press and it was just me being naïve again, to be honest. You hear celebrities moaning about how they carry on and that but it's not until you have dealings with them yourself that you get a real idea of what they're like. Basically, when I was up there on the crane, I was talking to a mate on the walkie-talkie and there was a guy from the Evening Standard. He had a word with me through the walkie-talkie and asked me if I had a photo of me and my ex and my daughter and offered me £300 or something for it. I said "Yes" because I thought my sister had got one, and then we started talking and before I knew where I was the next question was "Can you just confirm that you haven't got any drug convictions?" Well, I ain't gonna bullshit anyone and I said, "Yeah, I got a bit of puff a few years back, whatever," and that was it. That's all they wanted. The next thing I knew they did a piece about me and drugs. They had me. Still, if it's cheap tricks they want to get up to... it's bullshit basically. Nothing.

CHAPTER EIGHTEEN

In December 2003… no, no, I'm not going to start talking about Sarah's birthday party or anything. I mean, yes, December 15th is her birthday, but I've got nothing to do with that. I'm her dad.

As I said before, back in June I had been found guilty of harassing my ex. I had a three month curfew and an electronic tag put on me, and the reason I had been found guilty was that my solicitor said we couldn't use the tape I had of me talking to my ex about why she was doing what she was doing. She had claimed that I was threatening her and abusing her although the tape showed that it was actually the other way round. The solicitor had said that it was "inadmissible evidence". My solicitor told me - and I believed him - that it couldn't be used in the trial, but the solicitor I'd got in with the Spiderman protest said that it could have been used and that he'd be prepared to take my case on if I appealed. And it was shortly after that I found the tape could have been used and should have been used.

It was amazing that the solicitors told me it couldn't be used. What were they thinking? It beat me – these were supposed to be properly educated people, people with experience, people who knew what they were doing.

Why did I appeal? Hadn't I spent enough time fighting about in courts and banging my head against the wall? I appealed because even though you can't bring back time, even though you can't undo what's been done to you, right is right and wrong is wrong. And I was right and that… ex of mine was wrong. What happened in Kingston Court was actually funny. Well, it would have been funny if I hadn't already been through all that sick abuse and aggravation.

Before we'd even played him the tape, the judge stated that "he was doubtful of her evidence in chief" – a posh way of saying that he knew it was all bullshit. My ex was in the box, and already the judge was having serious reservations and doubting her bullshit. Me, I was in shock that there was a judge who seemed to know what he was doing.

"Does this first incident qualify as harassment?" he asked.

Of course it didn't. Once the tape was heard, it was all over. The conviction was effectively overturned. Then he says he'll take instructions in the light of what he's seen. That meant that he was giving her mob, the Crown Prosecution Service, the opportunity to back down. Then following a conference with the CPS, they say the words I wanted to hear. They said, "We're not in a position to proceed." My barrister made an application case of "no case to answer". CPS accepted it and was a total victory. We didn't even get to half-time and it was all over.

Judge Richard McGregor-Johnson also stated, "Mr Chick did not use the foul language or threats which Ms Green referred to in her statement. From her evidence in chief I was doubtful of her evidence."

When we came out of there, my ex had been exposed for what she was – a lying, deceitful… you know. She was in tears at the end, which was just as it should have been. What did she expect after all that? To be honest, it was a nice little buzz, because she deserved it after all that she's done to me and my daughter. But even though all that is true, I still felt that in a sense she got away with it because although the judge found against her, nothing was said about all the missed contacts, all the deliberate lies and the years that I'd been denied my daughter.

The problem was – and this is one of the big problems in

this whole story – that the Crown Court might have exposed Jan Green as a pathetic, lying perjurer, but when we got back in the Family Court it was back to the old story. The reason for that is that the Crown Court is open and the Family Court is behind closed doors and once you're behind closed doors they can do what they like, they can say what they like and no one can do anything about it.

Now with a case like mine, ordinarily the family courts would have had a problem backing down because this would mean they had to admit that they'd been wrong. And no one is going to stand up and admit that their organisation is corrupt at worst and incompetent at best. In a sense though I'd shot myself in the foot because now I was such a high profile case, there was no chance they were going to back down. No way. And in a Family Court with all the secrecy and closed doors, they didn't have to. For Cafcass to now do what was right for me and my daughter would be like them turning round and saying "We've done it wrong for the last three years. The whole Spiderman thing was all our fault". So, like all sorts of bullies, the big organisations stick together.

*　　*　　*　　*

Was I any further forward? I don't know. It was like they say, one step forward, two steps back. Basically I'd done a peaceful protest, I did the Spiderman protest, and still it was a year after that before I saw my daughter again. So I don't really think it helped in that. I'd become really high profile, I'd done everything properly, I'd been found not guilty by the Crown Court and yet… I still wasn't seeing Sarah. Despite having a fortnightly contact order during that whole time, no one said anything, no one did anything and Sarah was as far away as ever.

Who do I blame? Easy. The family law system. Despite me being convicted and serving a sentence without doing anything wrong, and despite her being proven to be lying, despite her perjuring herself in court, the Cafcass officer - David Irwin - still bullishly says that I'm the bad person and that he believes what she's saying. He still says that my ex's fears are justified. Despite any lack of concrete evidence or proof.

In a letter dated December 19th, he wrote: "In conclusion as to the parent's abilities in giving priorities to their daughter's welfare, I consider that Ms Green is successfully meeting that challenge. I believe that her expression of her distress is genuine and that she would be committed to Sarah's having a good relationship with her father. I consider that Ms Green is a sensible woman trying to do her best for her daughter. My personal experience of Mr Chick is of a quiet menace, quickly escalating into a confrontational attitude wherein any sensible discussion is impossible. If that is my experience, I must give credence to that of Ms Green. It seems to me that a major issue at the hearing of January 5th will be whether any contact should be resumed at the moment. Such contact could however only occur in the face of Ms Green clear opposition with the possible risks to her health and safety about which she is fearful. My view is that the court should give considerable weight to Ms Green views (which I consider to be valid). I consider that it is essential for Mr Chick to demonstrate at the next meeting that he can take a more reflective and balanced view of the situation before contact could take place."

So... everything she said is okay, everything I said was... of *quiet menace*. In the absence of proof and evidence on her part, I suddenly become a quiet menace. Not the raging, violent man of previous accusations. But suddenly a *quiet menace*. Can't get away with one thing, so we'll simply insinuate another. The power of words.

But didn't I have all the proof? Wasn't everything she said based on simply her word? Is it any wonder I was frustrated by this? Is it any wonder I expressed that? David

Irwin seemed to accept Jan's viewpoint from the off. It seemed from his report than anything Jan said about me or claimed about me would just be accepted. I wonder how 'confrontational' he'd be in attitude if he was sitting in my chair and I was sitting in his? And is this ex-probation officer, a man who receives less training than a traffic warden, some sort of psychiatrist now with his view of my quiet menace?

A more reasonable question might to ask whether Cafcass were not beginning to have it in for me? After all, I wasn't exactly spreading the word that they were a great organisation. I wasn't giving them any good publicity. I'd been stuck in the sky on a crane telling the world what a useless incompetent bunch they were. Was David Irwin just getting his own back?

Later that December I found out that the police were still investigating me. They didn't like me. Well, I'd caused them so much inconvenience with my protests and had come away from it – so far – reasonably unpunished. I can't think why they didn't like me. Quite a few of them made a good few bob on overtime. Maybe the ones I bumped into were coppers who didn't get a chance to ride on that gravy train. Maybe they were jealous.

I went on a Fathers 4 Justice Christmas demo. There were about 2,000 people there and we're all walking along, no grief like. I was dressed as Spiderman, a few others were in various outfits, a few were dressed up as Santa. It was peaceful and good-natured. We were walking along and I saw these two coppers watching me from about five to ten foot away. One of them came over to me and says, "Can you jump up on there for me I want to take a picture," and points to this wall about a two foot high. About as high as my knees. Stupidly and without thinking, I did. I forgot that one of my bail conditions after the Tower Bridge protest was not to climb any tall structures. Not that this was a tall structure.

"Right," he says. "Jump down now. You just broke your

bail conditions. You better watch yourself. We've got your card marked."

It was bullshit. All the times I got bail conditions I respected them and followed them. Even though I shouldn't have had them and even though it was all bullshit, I respected them because, basically, if I'd have broken them I'd have suffered.

This was bullshit and I didn't need that. I'd got enough shit in my head with all this nightmare to have the Old Bill playing tricks like that, it was bollocks. I put this little boy on my shoulder in case the old bill tried any other dirty tricks and I felt safer then. I was dressed in Spiderman, because I didn't have a condition that I couldn't dress up as Spiderman – yet. It was cute for the kid and offered protection for me. The Bill weren't going to mess with me with a kid on my shoulder.

You can't say all the coppers were this and that because I came across a lot of nice ones. Listen, the chances are that there were quite a few who were in my position, who were dads who weren't allowed to see their kids. They're only human, aren't they? A few times when I was walking past them in court and that, they'd give me a wink and quietly say to me "Nice one, some of us are with you" and things like that.

Meanwhile, I'd had another contact hearing at Guildford. It's important to have these things to let them know you're still there, that you haven't gone away. Contact hearing? It's stupid. You have a contact hearing so they can hear that there's been no contact. You make an application for these contact hearings and then you get one. You go there and you say that nothing's happened and then nothing happens. It just goes on forever. I suppose they earn a few bob out of it, but for the man in my position, it's nothing.

I also told the court that another bunch of solicitors had bitten the dust. Barnes and Partners never did jack shit while I was with them. I didn't get one hearing during that time.

These contact hearings, basically they don't do any good, but you've got to keep going with them to remind those slack incompetent bastards that you're still there. That no matter how much they close their eyes and wish you weren't there, well fuck it, no. I am here and I'm not going to go away. And you never know. One day you might turn up at a contact hearing and they'll say "Ah, Mr Chick. I do apologise but we've been wrong in the past..." That last bit's a joke. Then again, the whole thing's a joke. So the contact hearings, yeah. I apply for them when she's not complying with the contact order. I apply and the judge says whatever, but basically they do fuck all.

I though Barnes would be okay. The solicitor who helped me out when I did Spiderman put me on to this lot and he was a good lad, and I thought, well... But they weren't.

Surely there must be a good family solicitor out there who can do the right thing for my daughter and for me.

CHAPTER NINETEEN

It was funny. On the one hand I still had all the grief going on sacking solicitors, not seeing Sarah, grief from the ex, being treated like a twat by the police and the system. On the other hand I was voted second in the London Evening Standard Personality Of The Year 2003 awards. I came second to Roman Abramovitch, the owner of Chelsea football club, but I beat people like Jamie Oliver, Arsene Wenger and that twat Ken Livingstone. Basically, and I don't want to sound big-headed, but I'm pretty sure that they put someone in front of me just so that I wouldn't win. I don't see how I can beat Arsene Wenger but I can't beat Roman Abramovitch. I expect Abramovitch got a little medal or a pendant maybe - or a wallet – but it was nothing really.

I don't normally take much notice of stuff like that, but this was nice because it was voted for by the readers – it seemed that ordinary people were aware of what was right and what was wrong. At least they saw that I was doing some good. And all that effort by the police to get people pissed off with me by closing the roads and that, it didn't work. I didn't see the top cops who ordered all the roads to be closed up for any popularity awards.

I was also up for a Politician of the Year award - the Channel 4 viewers choice for "the person who made the most important contribution to British politics in 2003" and I made the final six. (Dr David Kelly won. The runners-up were Robin Cook, Tony Blair, George Galloway, Benjamin Zephaniah - and me. They said that viewers nominated me for "highlighting the scandalous way in which fathers get treated by the courts over contact with their children". Quite right too. That was freaky shit. I was up there with people like George Galloway and Tony Blair. Again that was a voter thing, the viewers, so that was good. They saw through all those police lies about he disruption I caused and that. You see, just like when I went to the Crown Court, when the people got a chance to speak they were all on my side. That's when people heard all the evidence. When it was the corrupt Cafcass people behind closed doors in the Family Courts, that's when I got shafted.

I went to the awards ceremony with Gemma. It was odd going to something like that, it's not the sort of thing I normally get invited to. It's not even the sort of thing I take much notice of. I've never been much interested in all that gossip showbiz stuff.

The bloke who plays Victor Meldrew and Ian Hislop were behind me, but you know where I am and whatever I do, my pain and my anger is always there. I can't forget why it is I'm there, what it is that's put me in that position and it always stops me enjoying myself because it really does my head in. This issue really does you. There's nothing more important than kids, and the pressure really does you. Whatever I do, it's always there. Every day, I wake up and I just want to see my kid. I don't know if it's going to be a month, a week, a year. I went 21 months without seeing her.

You can say that it's great that the public recognise what's going on. You can say that it must have been fun going to glamorous awards ceremonies or whatever. But I'm an ordinary bloke and want to be an ordinary bloke. And what I want is to see my girl.

What it meant to me though was that people recognised that what I was protesting about was important. It was a bit of a buzz seeing my name around in the papers and stuff for something other than doing a protest, but really I didn't care about any of that award stuff in itself. It was what it stood for that was important. You see, that's the difference between me and some of the other F4J people. I didn't want to be famous. I really did just want to see Sarah. I just wanted to be with her. Some other people, if they'd have been voted this or that, they'd have been on the phone and got themselves a manager and an agent and try and make it a career. Go on Big Brother or something.

David Ellison, F4J's international co-ordinator has said that a lot of F4J's success has been down to me, even though I've never been a member. Matt has never acknowledged that because it takes away some of his glory. In fact, he's blanked me to this day. I went up there to London just after Ron Davis did the "Funpowder Plot" – when he threw three condom's filled with purple coloured flour at the Prime Minister in the House of Commons on May 19th, 2004 - and I saw him there and he said, "E-mail me," and I thought maybe he would move on now, become a human being. But he still never got in touch. I took all his glory and he didn't like that. I think he'd fancied being voted top Personality Of the Year or whatever. I reckon he'd have loved to be voted one of the top six political figures in the country.

Not everyone thought I was so great though. In February I got a letter from some people called the Legal Services Commission because I'd just changed to my fifth firm of solicitors. It didn't mention in the letter that if they hadn't all been so useless I wouldn't have to change them. Basically they said that they're refusing my legal aid because I'm requiring my case to be conducted unreasonably. What does that mean? It means that they think I've incurred unnecessary costs. Come on. Be fair. The costs were only incurred because the solicitors kept screwing up.

On February 26th, I waited between Jan's mum's house and Sarah's nursery. I was missing Sarah so much I just wanted to get a glimpse of her. That's the thing with this 'system'. It plays with your human emotions so much that it turns you into something you're not. Makes you do things you'd rather not do. I also wanted to get a photo of her for me, yes, but also something to show my family what my daughter – their relative – looked like. I was just about to take a photo, but as Sarah walked towards me, Jan's mum saw me and put her hands over Sarah's face and that's what I ended up with: a photo of Jan's mum's hands covering Sarah's face. What a lovely woman. What harm would it have done to let me have a photograph of my daughter? Honestly, by what right has anyone got to stop me seeing what my own daughter looks like?

*   *   *   *

The way I look at it, I'm trying to get enforced what the court has said. The court said that I should be able to see my daughter in the contact centres and no one has been able to make that happen. All the solicitors are so shit. This new firm that I've got hold of – van Baaren & Wright of London – seem reasonable and look at though they might be different. But I've thought that before. We'll see. I wrote a letter back explaining the story so far, what had happened and, more to the point, what hadn't happened. Shortly after I got a letter stating that legal aid had been re-granted.

So far I'd spent over £25,000 in actual money spent, and if you include the amount of money I've lost through not being able to work, this whole thing has cost me about £70,000. And still the courts won't make her pay up a claim of £2,000 I've had outstanding since we split up. It's been going on and going on and every time she was ordered to pay it she… just ignored it. Like she did with the orders to go to the contact centres.

In March 2004 there was another hearing about this £2,000 and she didn't turn up, she just wrote this very nice sounding letter, all "I'm so terribly sorry", all that. These words that sound great, but don't mean anything. I'm a nice I just forgot. Please don't make me pay the £2,000. It worked. She didn't.

The trial at Southwark Crown Court where I was facing a charge of causing a public nuisance went okay too. There was loads of stuff in the papers and on the telly at the time saying that I'd cost the country up to £40million by going up that crane, that because all the roads had to be closed (had to???) so much business was lost and it was all my fault. Well, it wasn't. They found me Not Guilty. Not that the trial was without its ups and downs.

Shortly after the trial started the judge said that Legal Aid for me to be represented by a QC has been refused. Great. Even the prosecutor said that he'd never heard of a case starting and then for the judge to question the involvement of a QC. Thankfully, my QC Nadine Radford said that she'd like to be paid but if necessary would do the case pro-bono – for free.

The actual details of the trial were a farce. The top police who'd authorised all the road closures weren't even called to appear and were willing to let lower ranked coppers defend their dirty work. And I'm not surprised. I knew the truth about the police's tactics would come out, and it did. A note written by Superintendent Tom Henley said that the closures should be used as a "bargaining tool" with Mr. Chick. It said, "Climber does not like road closures, so should be used as a bargaining tool against you and your cause". He signed off by saying: "My decision ... leave the roads closed."

Another police record said Tower Bridge "could be reopened if required" but pointed out its continued closure "could help in negotiations". And on the fifth day of the protest, an officer wrote there was "a possibility of weakening the prosecution case by opening the roads".

The prosecution case was extremely selective. Most of their time seemed to be spent outlining the conditions that would be placed on me should I be found guilty:

1)   I am not to carry out a public demonstration alone or with others from or on any building or structure which is man made or natural or other above the height of two metres above ground or water level.

2)   I am not to trespass on land belonging to any person whether legal or natural within England or Wales.

3)   I am not to enter or to be found in the London borough of Tower Hamlets.

4)   I am not to display myself in a fashion/manner which is likely to cause disruption or inconvenience to any other person.

5)   I am not to assault, abuse, threaten, harass, intimidate or act in such a manner as to cause distress to any person.

6)   I am not to incite another person to demonstrate on my behalf.

I made a note of all those conditions because it just summed it all up to me. The police knew that I was innocent because it was them that was guilty. There was no question. There were all the written records. But instead of apologising – or even building a proper defence – they were so arrogant that they put their time and energy into worrying about what they were going to do to me after I'd been convicted.

It was all such nonsense and I was obviously not guilty of what they were accusing me of. The trial lasted for ten days and at the end of it all there was one thing that bothered me. If there had been all this money lost because of the road closures, if that had caused a public nuisance and if I wasn't guilty then surely the police who had authorised that action should have been charged?

The other thing, were they going to prosecute every project that caused a disruption? What about when they transported the crane there in the first place? Didn't that cause a disruption? It was all bullshit. Most of the prosecutions case was based on a health and safety 'expert' who wasn't an expert at all. He thought that "Spiderman" could shift huge weights on the crane, which was obvious nonsense. There was no logic in the police's actions about first closing the roads and then re-opening them. I proved that I was not violent; that I didn't do anything that was obscene or offensive, that I was just exercising my right to free speech and peaceful protest. That was what got me off in the end, that line about this country prides itself on freedom of speech.

The jury of five men and seven women at Southwark Crown Court also heard extracts from police logs that made it clear that senior police officers not only treated the road closures as a 'bargaining tool' to get me to come down, but also worried that the case against me could be 'weakened' if they were lifted. I was just a desperate man who wanted to see his daughter and here they were, trying to blame me for a situation entirely of their own making.

I was asked what I was going to say when it ended. What was I going to say? Was it going to talk about British justice and my true faith in the legal system?

The day after the trial ended, May 14th, I went up to Norwich with Gemma because there was a family party for her grandfather's birthday. Halfway through the day I had an idea. I nipped out of the house and drove 40 miles down the road to Ipswich where there was a football match Ipswich v West Ham that was live on Sky TV. Time for Spiderman to make a quick appearance. I'd had all these conditions put on me for the past few months – I couldn't do this and I couldn't do that – but that finished now and I just wanted to let the authorities know that I wasn't going to go away.

It was a bit of a rush job, a bit Mickey Mouse compared to the proper protests. When I got there I couldn't get a ticket so I waited outside till half time and saw a couple of Ipswich guys going across the road for a pint. I told them I needed to get in and why I wanted to get in. They said walk in with us. When the game started I made my way down to the front, shoved my hood on and went onto the pitch. But when I shoved the hood on, I didn't get my eyeholes right so I couldn't see where I was going too well. Still it did a job. Basically I wanted to show the authorities that here I am.

CHAPTER TWENTY

Despite my new status as legal expert, despite me having done time representing myself, despite me spending more time in court since this lark began than your average judge, despite all that, the ways of the legal industry still baffled and amazed me. There's been a story rumbling on ever since I moved out of the house, a lifetime ago, about my possesions that she was keeping and the compensation I was supposed to get. I'd claimed £2,000 – a figure based on actual things that she had, goods of mine. She'd originally counterclaimed for a similar amount – a figure based on nothing and her wish not to pay what I was owed – before amending her counterclaim, over a year later, to £7,000. It was typical of the sort of thing she did. Petty and spiteful. This story had been rumbling on since autumn 2001 and it was now March 2004. Finally the story came to an end at a "chattels hearing" at Guildford. The result? The judge ordered her to give me a mirror back. Okay, it was my mirror and I wanted it, but how many court hearings? How many solicitor's letters? How much money wasted? How much time spent? And at the end of it… a mirror. It beat me. Still, it keeps people employed I guess.

I made an application to have our case transferred to the Royal Courts of Justice – the place known to fathers everywhere as "Heartbreak Hotel" after the old Elvis song. I basically requested that Judge Critchlow be taken off our case because of all the judgements he'd made in the past which I hadn't been too impressed with, and that request was granted. Finally I thought we might be getting somewhere. After asking and trying for what seems like years – it probably was – my family case was transferred to the High Court.

The first one we go to in June, Jan didn't show up. At first I thought, "How can she just not turn up? This is the High Court. This is proper." But then again, you look back at any of the things that she's done and you could ask, "How can she?" But it was good because there was an order put on her that if she didn't turn up the following month, she could – at the very worst – be put in prison. But they'd never done that when she didn't bother to turn up to any of the contacts over the years so it shows you what they think is more important - her turning up at court or me seeing my daughter.

The Family Court system is useless and helps no one. People can get away with all sorts of rubbish behaviour – as my ex has proved. In the High Courts you've got to believe that things are going to be taken a bit more seriously. So I thought. The first one we had booked, she didn't bother to turn up. It was just like it had always been.

BUT she did turn up the following month on the 28th but that was only because they attached a subpoena notice saying that you've got to come to this or you go to prison. If they do that, she'll turn up, but they never do that regarding contact which they could have done. It's funny, you know, but it strikes me that this is something they could have done right at the beginning that could have saved me and Sarah all this grief. And thinking about it I don't know why they don't do this for everyone in our situation.

The Family Court system doesn't work. So why not just issue subpoenas to all these mothers who abuse the system and disregard the court orders by not turning up to the contacts? Can you imagine what would have happened to the ex of mine if, the first time she failed to show up for a contact – Sarah's ill – she had a subpoena slapped on her head? That would have been the end of that wand this would have been a very short book. In fact, I wouldn't have had to write it.

After three years we were given a Cafcass legal officer, Elisabeth Major, rather than a normal run-of-the-mill Cafcass officer. Maybe it's because we've gone from the Family Court to the High Court. (Elisabeth Major was supposed to be Sarah's 'guardian'. Excuse me, I thought I was Sarah's guardian? Oh well.) Now that we're a high profile story they need a high profile person in charge. Somehow by going up a crane I became a more important person and they were concerned that I keep quiet. But they knew what to do to keep me quiet – just do right by me and my daughter, but they didn't do that. They thought they could get away with what they did in the secret Family Courts. But I am one person whose child they shouldn't nick because I was going to come after them. The Royal Courts Of Injustice is still held behind closed doors. It's the same as the old Family Courts. A more impressive building but the same old secrets.

She was supposed to be an expert, so I decided to give her the benefit of the doubt because, well, you've got to. If something new comes along you've got to give it a chance. But at the same time I knew that however good or whatever this legal officer was, the chances that they'd turn round and say that Cafcass has been incompetent and corrupt... It's not going to happen. Still, if she really is an expert, she'll soon realise what's been going on in this case. She'll soon see.

If Elisabeth Major really was an expert, she must have come across these stories before. She must have come across people behaving like this before. It's inconceivable that she hadn't seen the tricks and games. But they truth is that these people don't give a toss. They say they do, but they don't. One minute they're saying: "Mr Chick's commitment to his daughter cannot be questioned," that I'm the best dad in the world, but at the same time they're not seeing things that are staring them in the face. And what "she (the mother) says" always overrides factual things that are indisputable and are staring them in the face.

At the next contact hearing at the Royal Courts Of Justice on July 28, we got Judge Munby. Now he was supposed to be a top man so I thought maybe I'd have a chance of something proper. Some chance. He'd made a bit of a name amongst the disaffected fathers groups after writing in April 2004 about another case he was ruling on: "From the father's perspective the last two years of the litigation have been an exercise in absolute futility. When his counsel told me that the father felt very let down by the system, I was not surprised. I can understand why he expresses that view. He has every right to express that view. In a sense it is shaming to have to say it, but I personally agree with his view. It is very, very disheartening."

Elisabeth Major reported (on July 2nd) and said that because Sarah and I had been apart for so long, we should be referred to a specialist agency, Baker and Duncan, for assessment. Baker and Duncan Family Consultancy, to give them their full title, are a firm of expert child psychiatrists who specialise in cases like ours where's there's been a major gap in the contact and where everyone might need a bit of expert advice in the early stages. It's only a small firm, but they're supposed to be the top people. It was something. Then, in the recommendations part of her report, it said "In the meantime, the order for contact dated December 18, 2002, be suspended".

Judge Munby agreed and ordered "contact be suspended". Great. It was 16 months after Jan had unofficially suspended contact and here was the court making it official. I understood that their reasoning, that it had been so long since Sarah and I had seen each other that we needed assistance to re-start our relationship when we got back together again. It could be quite traumatic for a little girl to be presented with this bloke after such a long absence and be told, "He's your dad". Especially when in all likelihood she'd been fed all sorts of lies and hateful stories about me by my ex. In some respects, they were probably protecting me – but maybe I was just beyond desperate by now and clinging onto anything I could view as a positive.

I could understand that we needed assistance of some sort. What I couldn't understand was why that meant we had to have contact suspended. Surely we should just be getting on with it. Now. Was he not just making Jan's actions official? She'd 'suspended contact' 16 months ago. No one had said anything to her and here he was, the top man, in a sense making it official.

As Munby was making his judgement, I saw a spider doing what it has to do.

*   *   *   *

Every time something changed, there was a small part of me that thought, "This is it. This is the thing that changes it." We move from the Family Court with its behind closed doors secrecy and corrupt officers to the open and transparent High Court. I thought that was it. Now she'll be forced to comply with the courts. Didn't happen. She abused a flawed system just as she always had done.

Then we got a legal officer from Cafcass rather than the ordinary officer we'd had. I thought that might change things, that this new turbo-charged, high-power legal officer would have the brains to see through her bullshit. Didn't happen. It was still the same old "Mother knows best" crap.

Then we went up in front of a bloke who was supposedly the top man, Judge Munby. He was supposed to be the one. And what did this amazing bloke say? This man who's supposed to be one of the top legal minds in the country, what did he say? He said that in order for me and Sarah to get to know each other, contact would be officially suspended! What an idiot. This was just playing into her hands. She'd suspended contact ages ago. When was the last time I'd seen Sarah? What this judge should have done was thrown the law at my ex. She'd been taking the piss out of it for years and no one had ever held her to account. This judge, that's what he should have done. Instead he does the same as she's been doing. He suspends contact. Basically, he says to her "What's you've done is okay. I'll save you the bother now and make it official".

It seemed like every time I did a protest something would happen and then… nothing would happen. They'd throw a scrap in the hope that it would make me go away. But nothing actually changed. It was all just surface stuff and it got on my tits as much as if they'd done nothing at all. And then when Munby said that contact was suspended…

I like doing things like cranes. As a peaceful protest I think it's perfect. You get up there, you make your statement and no one can touch you. No one can control you – you control the whole situation. When I went up on the cranes, I knew that there was virtually no chance of my protest finishing before I chose to end it. And when I was thinking of the next protest, that's the sort of thing I was thinking of.

I want to do something that was in that sense the same, but which was different – bigger and better. The London Eye was perfect. A huge structure bang in the centre of London. Officially the world's highest observational wheel. Once I was up there, no one would be able to miss me and no one would be able to stop me.

I'd been up The Eye twice in my life before, and I'd been there a month before to check out how I could get up and on and worked out how to get in. Basically, there was this ladder that went all the way round and that seemed to be the way. There were a few obstacles to overcome: a Perspex wall about 10 feet designed to stop people getting in and a few security guards around the place, chatting or whatever.

Nothing for Spiderman to worry about. It was a bit harder for David Chick, but we'd get there. I got in there and then worked my way round some mechanical bits and pieces, up a few stairs and then found my way onto a spiral staircase that was used by the maintenance people. I had a look at it, the door to the spiral staircase was open so that was that. In we go.

September 11, 2004. I got there at about midnight and waited till it was really quite, about 4am. I'd managed to get over this perspex wall thing and there's a couple of security guards down there, chatting away. I managed to get onto the wheel and they shouted to me:

"Hey, what you doing?"

I looked down and shouted back, "Maintenance" and just carried on.

I got through this gate, chucked my bag round, went up a couple of stairs, got onto the mechanism and up onto the ladder. I'd got to about 7 O Clock on the wheel when this major light was turned on. I looked round and it was the police.

"We could shoot you," they shouted up. It was the anniversary of 9:11.

It was a total coincidence. People have asked me if there was something significant in the fact that it was September 11. And it was. It was significant because it was the day I went up the London Eye protesting about the state-sponsored abuse of my relationship with my daughter. Nothing else. Do I look like a fundamentalist Muslim? It had nothing to do with the attack on New York or anything. It was totally coincidental on my part. I kicked myself for seizing an opportunity and not checking the date first. Looking back, there was more risk of being shot which would have been pointless; I want to be there for my daughter.

I had some press advisors and, actually I was going to do the protest the weekend before, but they said, "Don't do it this weekend," because the Olympics was on. They said to me that if I did it that weekend I'd get no press coverage. They cancelled it and made me do it on the anniversary of 9/11. they didn't realise it was the anniversary of 9/11 or maybe they did, Maybe they did and wanted me to get fucking shot, I don't know. It sure would have been a great story. They said they'd done a deal with the News of the World and it'll bring in a few quid, but they didn't.

This was without doubt the most dangerous protest I'd done. I was determined to stay up there for 18 hours because it was 18 months since I'd seen my little girl and I wanted it to be significant. But it was fucking hard. I got up to the top - 450 feet up in the air. Saying it like that makes me worse than actually being up there. 450 feet. It's a long way up. When you're looking down on trees and birds flying around, you know you're a long way up. I haven't got a problem with heights particularly – wouldn't be much good as Spiderman if I was scared as heights. It would be like Batman not liking caves - but it was incredibly windy up there. It was also the tail end of a hurricane and it was blowing like mad. It wasn't that cold. No, it could have been warmer and I didn't have that much clothing with me because whatever I had I had to carry, but it was the strength of the wind that was doing me in.

The other thing was that I had no walkie-talkies. I didn't have any real mates there and there was no support. That didn't bother me because I'd always done them by myself in the past. The only time that other people have known exactly what I was doing was the Tower Bridge one. But I'd had so little help and support from F4J since then, just hostility from Matt, that I didn't trust them anymore. I thought, "Right, I'll do it myself." I didn't even want to tell them, just in case some muppet leaked it out.

I took up the usual stuff – you've got to remember I knew this story by now. I knew what to do. I only had one holdall and a big banner. On one side the banner said "In The Name Of The Children" and on the other it said "Failed and abused by Family Law".

The whole thing wasn't great really. When I got to the top I found that there was no access to the cabins. They were all sealed up and there was nowhere to chill out. There was nowhere indoor to escape. At least with the cranes, you've got the driver's cabin, but here there was nothing. I had thought that I'd be able to get on the top and have a little lie down, but there was nowhere to grab hold of, nowhere to relax. It really was quite dangerous.

I came down that night when I'd done what I wanted to do. I said I'd do 18 hours and that was good enough for me. When I came down I was arrested again – of course – and as always they took me off. This time though they refused me bail. They had no grounds to do that but just to piss me off, they did. I was bailed the next day, on the 13th, with the following conditions. I wasn't to enter London, I couldn't put on my Spiderman outfit or do anything a little bit spidery – no webs or anything, you know – and I had to sleep every night at my home address.

There was a bit of press and I made a statement - "My protest has moved forward, and has had to move forward, because nothing has changed to right the wrongs of one parent blocking an ex-partner access to their children in defiance of a court order. I am not a troublemaker or attention seeker, but the British justice system has completely failed my child and I. To those who have been inconvenienced by my protest, I apologise." Most of the press was again because the pictures looked so great. Spiderman on top of the London Eye over the London skyline was a great image, so there was stuff in the Sunday papers. There wasn't much of a follow up because the next day Jason Hatch from Fathers 4 Justice went into Buckingham Palace and did a protest on the balcony. It was nothing to do with me. I didn't know anything about it. (I didn't like all that. I'm a serious protestor and this is a serious thing. The men who climbed up Buckingham Palace were seen laughing and goading the police. I wouldn't diminish my protest by acting in that way.) It got Matt a lot of press and that was nice for him I guess and he said that their protest was timed to coincide with the trial of Ron Davis and the Funpowder Plot guys.

The Buckingham Palace protest was a good choice for headlines. It was front page news because it's the Queen's house but there's no duration to it and that's important to me. It was the same with the flour bombers in Parliament. Anyone can do something for a minute but sticking it out, that's what counts. If you stick it out, if you show that you're prepared to hang in there, that shows you're serious, that you're prepared to do what it takes. The longer you do it, even though you don't get the front page, there's a lot more thought. I could do the Queen or the Houses of Parliament, but I prefer to do things that have got a bit more duration, that show a bit more determination. Also you've got to remember that F4J, that's an organisation. I'm not an organisation, I'm just one man acting alone.

Sometimes it seems to me that the whole of my life has been taken over by this business. There never seems to be a week where there isn't something happening. There never seems to be a time when something isn't happening. Yeah, it was happening but what still wasn't happening was contact. Oh no, sorry, I forgot. There couldn't be contact. That would be against the law. The Judge said so.

Still, it wasn't only me who was going through this. Thousands of fathers all over the world are going through the same thing. You've only got to look on the internet to see how many people are struggling. I've got a similar situation to mine a little bit closer to home than some internet website: my brother. Strange isn't it. My brother is going through almost the same shit as I'm going through although, in fairness he gets a much better deal than I do. His ex-wife is pretty much the same as mine but not as severe. Mad but not as mad.

My brother's got three sons – twins aged 11 and another two years older - and gets to see them fairly regularly. As a situation it's not perfect but you know, you live with situations if you think it's as good as you're going to get. And my brother's not going to do anything that might send his ex over the edge because he's seen what's happened to me. He knows how easy it would be for his ex to turn round and… that would be it. When would he see his sons again? I used to see my nephews quite a lot and we used to have a good text relationship. I'd pick them up from school and stuff. It was sweet as.

On September 22 I was arrested and charged with harassment of my nephews. My ex-sister in law saw a text to them one day, and the next thing I know I'm arrested and charged with harassment. She's not so different from my ex. She sent me a text which said, "Just because you can't see your children, don't ruin your brother's contact." It was a familiar old story. She had no proof and no evidence. I had loads of proof and loads of evidence - letters from all three of my nephews saying that we had a good relationship, loads of videos footage collected over the years that showed how well we all got on. Of course it didn't matter. I'm a bloke, she's a woman. And we know that these things aren't done in the child's best interests, they're done in the interests of the mother". My brother had stuck up for me and argued my case but what can he do? He wants to see his kids. As it was she punished him and cancelled a contact. He had it down that he saw his kids once during midweek and at every other weekend, and during this period she cancelled the midweek contact. Just like that. Is she allowed to do that? Haven't you been paying attention? She's the mother: she's allowed to do what she likes.

I was released with bail conditions about me not contacting my nephews, not getting in touch with my ex sister in law directly – like I would want to – and there's another condition on top of that: I wasn't allowed to enter Brighton until September 30th. There was a Labour Party conference on that week. Maybe the court thought I was going to throw a web around the Brighton Centre.

The whole thing was ridiculous, so much of what had gone on – what was still going on - was ridiculous. Looking back, I think I was paying the price for being David Chick. The system doesn't like it when someone stands up and says that they're not going to take it anymore. That's the last thing the system wants and I was someone who stood up. I was seen as trouble and it wasn't just that the system couldn't let me be seen to win or get away with it. The system had to slap me down. If it didn't, it would encourage other people to stand up, wouldn't it? I think the other thing that was going on was what Jan had been working towards for years: the drip… drip… effect. Jan has thrown so many accusations at me over the years, made so many claims that after a while people started to think "There's got to be something in it". It doesn't matter that she's never had any evidence, it doesn't matter that she's been proved in the High Court to be a liar and a perjurer. It's that thing that if you say something enough times, people will listen.

The result of all this was that I was in court in September and October for this case and both times they said that they were thinking of dropping the case against my three nephews. It eventually took them nine months to do it and in that time I wasn't able to talk to my nephews, I couldn't text them, couldn't speak to them, couldn't see them. Is that in the child's best interests? I love them and want to see them. They love me and want to see me. And remember all this was on no evidence, just the word of my ex sister-in-law. Simple as that.

CHAPTER TWENTY-ONE

November 2004. It's now over 20 months since Sarah and I have had any contact. When Judge Munby made his judgement that contact being officially suspended, he recommended that it be resumed in October. Well, need I even bother to say that it didn't happen in October? I didn't happen in November either. Why didn't anything happen? I really don't know. The judge said that he wanted first contact in October but actually the first one was in December, December 7th. Also, I should say that we had our first meeting with Baker and Duncan on September 17th but the follow-up the next week was cancelled because... Jan couldn't make it.

Despite the ruling from Judge Munby about saying that contact had to be suspended because we needed assistance and coaching because we hadn't seen each other for so long, we didn't get any coaching. Another big surprise. Basically the judge had stopped Sarah and me seeing each other for a few months for no reason. Well, there was a reason but they'd gone back on it, like they did with everything. In fairness, what I think must have happened was that Sarah had been going to this experts centre and getting familiar with one of the women who worked there, so she was like friendly and she trusted this woman. So the idea as that woman would bring her into the contact and pass her on to me and that way Sarah would know that I was okay. I understood all that, but it was still gutting. Couldn't I have been part of that process? How did it make me feel, that my daughter had to be made to think I was okay by some strange woman.

How did it make me feel? It made me feel like a father in the system – basically nothing. I got no advice from Cafcass. No advice, no assistance, no help. It was just "You're going to see Sarah on this day for an hour and it's going to be videoed". That was it basically. The video was for the court and the mother to see how I was with my daughter. I mean she gets all that but did I ever get a video to see how she was with my daughter? Don't be stupid. It just runs along with it all. Basically the message always is: fathers you might as well just piss off and kill yourself. Being videoed, it makes you feel like you're on trial. But then again, I've been on trial these past however many years. Despite doing everything right.

Did I get any support at all on any level about anything at all? Don't be stupid.

I'd built up this meeting into something so big yet in truth I wasn't even sure that she'd be there. Sure, Jan had been told that she must attend, but how many times had she been told that? Even in itself, that uncertainty was too much. I don't know how I'd have reacted if she hadn't turned up. Probably I wouldn't have been surprised.

Baker and Duncan's assessment was that we were to have six contacts, once a fortnight, to see how it was going. Based on those contacts and the reports, progress would be made. We'd move forward. Things would change. Their first report did contain one line that went down my spine: "Sarah refers to Mr Chick as 'her other daddy'." Another thing it said was "Any intimate care of Sarah, e.g. taking to the toilet, would be conducted by Dr Petch-Hill. Mr Chick may want to bring games, food, snacks and drinks to the contact". Any intimate care would be conducted by someone else? How sad is that?

Interestingly, Baker and Duncan's report contained the following paragraph which seemed to sum up the situation well: "If the court believes that Sarah would be best placed with the father on the basis that the mother has maliciously and deliberately and purposely created a web of lies in conspiring and in collusion with her parents to create a situation in which Mr Chick has been deliberately excluded from Sarah's life, then the court may conclude that this is tantamount to very serious emotional abuse which would warrant the child's removal and placement with the father."

The contacts that we were supposed to have were to take place at their centre in Brookwood, near Woking in Surrey. They had initially suggested weekly meetings, but Jan said that that would be too difficult to commit to as it would wipe the whole afternoon away, her running her own business and that. Naturally, they said "OK". It's strange that even these experts, even these specialists considered the interests of Jan's business concerns over the interests of a child re-building a relationship with her father. What was that line from the Government act again? In the child's best interests. Why suddenly had that changed to "in the mother's interests"? Or, better still, "In the mother's best business interests"?

That first contact, an hour meeting, on December 7th was completely freaky, the strangest feeling I've ever had. Can you imagine how nervous I was? Nervous, excited... everything. I didn't know what to feel. I didn't know what to wear even. Everything inside me was just so tense. This was what I'd been building for the last two years. My little girl. I hadn't seen her for 21 months. What was she going to be like? What was she going to look like? What would she sound like? I'd seen her twice from a distance – breaking the rules, I know, but sometimes you've just got to do it, you know? I followed her twice to a playground on February 26th 2004 and April 23rd 2004. I didn't approach her or anything, I'm not that stupid, but I got a glimpse of her at the nursery playground. Just a couple of times. I don't know, sometimes it just got too much for me. I sat in my car and looked at her and in some ways that was harder than not seeing her at all. Being so close, being so near to her and not being able to touch her or call out to her. Apart from that sneaky stuff, I hadn't seen any pictures of her, no videos of her, nothing.

How did it go? I dunno. A lot of it, you don't have to be taught how to be. If you're a good decent person, it's just going to come naturally. You know what's right for your kids whether they're two or 20. You know how to behave. I know how to behave with my daughter, without my daughter. I do everything right all the time. At the contact centre when she first came into the room, she was with this woman from this expert organisation. In two years she had changed a lot. Her hair had grown, she'd got a bit taller, but I dunno, she was still my little girl.

And after being apart from her for so long, it's difficult to talk. Mostly when you talk to someone, you're talking about things that you both know about. You talk about what you've been up to and there's a way of talking together that you're used to. It's hard with very young kids anyway, and when you haven't seen someone for a while... It is hard. Mostly during these contacts it wasn't really talking. We did a bit of colouring, a bit of playing. It was just all about being close to each other rather than actual talking, just spending time in each other's company, laughing and being together. But you know, you're in this place that means nothing to either of you with these people watching your every move. It's about as bad as you can get. The only worse thing is no contact at all and when you've had that, mate you're so happy to have this.

I watched her and thought about all the shit that I've been through these last two years just to see my little girl. I just wanted to go and give her a cuddle but I knew I had to take my time. I knew that to go straight to her would be more damage than good after all that's been going on for 21 months. I had to be contained, and as much as I wanted to give her a kiss and a cuddle and all that I had to control myself. But that's just the shit that you have to go through.

Sarah looked around and saw me. She grabbed on to the woman she was with and it was obvious she was fearful of me from what she'd been told – that was hard to take. The whole thing was fantastically difficult. Not only had we not seen each other for so long. Not only were we in this contact centre. Not only was there a supervisor keeping an eye on us. But we were being videoed. It was like I was on trial. Big Brother watching what I was doing. Checking up to see whether I was good enough. Good enough to warrant another contact.

But it was great. They gave me a copy of the video and you can see it. Kids are instinctive, they're good at picking up the vibes and you can really see it. After that first five minutes or so, which were tense, she was laughing and it was obvious she saw me for what I am and not this bullshit. She was playing, she was happy. It was beautiful and sweet, but at the same time it made me feel fucking sick at all the time we'd lost, all the time we'd had stolen. At the end we kissed and cuddled and she waved goodbye when she went.

The psychiatrists, who were shown the video and had to make a report on it, said that I was contained and containing and was entirely appropriate with my daughter, not rushing her, not crowding her, giving her space and dealing with her very sensitively. There was nothing about this contact, they said, that was in any way concerning on the part of the daughter or father.

We had two more contacts on January 4th and January 18th and it was lovely to see Sarah, I can't tell you. It's very hard in that bland sterile environment, and when you've only got an hour with them it's very difficult to get close. An hour every two weeks?

*　　*　　*　　*

Contact – that word still sticks in my throat – was going well. Baker and Duncan were happy. The experts were happy. Sarah was happy. Obviously it was time for Jan to throw a spanner and she did something that really was very nasty.

When it was me against her, I knew she'd play dirty and, in a way, I can understand that. Couples split up, they get bitter, they get angry with each other and they try to hurt each other. That's what happens. It's standard. But, for me, using your child as a weapon in all that is totally out of order. You don't do it. You don't mess about with the mind of a young kid just to hurt someone else. I don't understand how anyone can do that. But there was a lot I didn't understand. I could understand why Jan would want to be Sarah's primary parent. That's what I wanted so I could understand why she'd want it too. But I couldn't understand why she wanted to – from Day One – wipe me and Sarah out of each other's lives. That, to me, was unfathomable. What was also unfathomable to me was using a young child's mind to get at and hurt someone you were having a row with.

Basically, the story is this. I'd put in a claim for residency because I didn't want my little girl to be brought up by my ex. She'd proved herself to be incompetent as a mother; she'd proved herself to be a bad mother. Parents are supposed to be moral guardians and what sort of moral example had she been setting? Anyway, just before our first scheduled contact – December 7th – Jan told Sarah that I wanted full-time residence. She told her that I wanted to take her away. Okay, Sarah might have been my daughter and we might have loved each other and that but we hadn't seen each other for two years. Half her life. Not only that, but all she'd heard about me in those last two years was that I was a monster, that I was nasty, that, I don't know, had a couple of horns and a tail.

To tell a four-year-old child that this man wants to take

her away from Mummy, what's that about? So you can imagine a four-year-old girl being thrilled by this news? That's
inflicting unnecessary shit on a little child, yeah? About this
point, Baker and Duncan wrote, "We must assume that
Sarah has been made aware of Mr Chick's residence application [by Jan]." We must assume? What other possibility
was there? That Sarah picked up some correspondence and
read it herself?

The upshot of that application for residency was a three-
day hearing at the Royal Courts Of Justice in front of Judge
Munby. The first day was set for December 20th 2004, five
days after Sarah's birthday. I'd tried to get Judge Munby
moved from our case because after his decision last time we
were up against him (when he said that contact should be
officially suspended because Sarah and me hadn't seen each
other for so long) any confidence I had in him as a judge and
a human being had gone. Jan wanted him to stay put and
given his attitude to us, I can't say I'm surprised she wanted
that. He stayed. Of course he stayed. What mother wants...

We'd gone in with a 'Position Statement' from my
barrister saying what we wanted and why it should be
agreed to and, you know, we could point to my ex's attitude
and behaviour and all the lies and deceit. I'd been quite
hopeful that this would be positive because by now she'd
been shown up in the high court to be a liar and I'd been
shown in that December 7th contact video to be normal and
proper and nothing like she'd said.

The court proceedings got under way. My solicitors, the
psychiatrist, the Cafcass legal officer, and Jan, they came back
and said that we should go along with what they're saying
because there was no point in going for residence. They'd
suggested nine months of managed contact and to try and
fight this would be to risk not seeing Sarah for years. I
wouldn't get residence, they said, because Sarah doesn't
know you. No judge is going to give grant residence in those
circumstances, they said, because she doesn't even know

her daddy. Yes, Jan was in there, she was involved in that discussion. I wasn't involved. I wasn't invited. I had my representation in there so I was only aware of what my solicitor told me, while Jan was in there. She had it all first hand, and she had the chance to tell them all what I was "really" like. I don't understand why. Where's the impartiality in that?

They said, "Let's wait until she's at ease with you and then we'll go for residence." The Position Statement said that as soon as Sarah was comfortable with me, we'd have overnight stays and more contact, and the hearing agreed with that. But, of course, that would be more time wasted and more time for Jan not to turn up and more time for her to fill Sarah's head with her vicious lies.

The case was adjourned. We didn't even use the second and third days. Why did the solicitors buy that? We got a three-day hearing, which apparently you never get at the Royal Courts of Justice and then they said, "We don't want those other two days". But you know why? They said to me, don't rock the boat Dave. Be happy with this. The reality was though that this "victory" left with a paltry 25% of the contact that was first ordered all those years ago. Back then, I was supposed to get two hours every Saturday, this was an hour per fortnight. That's progress?

The good thing that came out of it was that they had this discussion; my solicitors came back to me and said that Cafcass have said if she doesn't start complying with this contact order, she's been told that she's at risk of losing residence. I'm not sure I believe it. I'm not sure that they'd force it, but that's why she turns up on the dot now every fucking time. It forces Jan to do what she's supposed to do. At the end of the day they all know what she's fucking done. But they can't turn around and do the right thing and admit that because that would mean admitting their liability.

Is this a result? Because finally Jan is being forced to do what she's supposed to have been doing for years, is this a result for Sarah and me? But even after all this time, even after everything's that's happened, she still gets everything. The courts still call in her favour, Cafcass still loads everything in her favour and you get the impression that they always will. It doesn't seem to matter what the father says or does, it doesn't matter how badly a mother behaves, they still think that because she's the mother she must be right.

In February I was finally granted parental responsibility, the best part of four years after I applied for it. Parental responsibility means that you're entitled to know basic things about your child like her health and her school. Where her doctor is, where she goes to school. What her health records say. Just the normal general things that any parent should be entitled to know about their child. If I'd have had parental responsibility in the beginning would she have been able to get away with missing all those contacts with her "Sarah's ill" bullshit? Probably because she gets away with everything, but it might have been harder. Anyway, even when I was granted this thing, it was still another four months before I actually got it.

When it was granted, I asked - because I wanted to know - about Sarah's new school and her doctor, but Baker and Duncan told me to go Elisabeth Major, Sarah's guardian at Cafcass who then went to Jan and asked her if she would allow me to have that information. Excuse me, I've got an order from the courts and you're still checking with her if I can have this information? Again, despite a court order, I was still being viewed as a third class citizen. And not getting what was mine.

On March 7th, Jan wrote to my solicitors: "At present I will not be providing the details of Sarah's nursery and general practitioner's. If there are any concerns regarding Sarah's health or schooling enquiries may be made through Cafcass." Jan didn't need a solicitor. She had Cafcass doing that job for her. How did she get away with it? I don't know.

If I had this parental responsibility, why could she refuse to give me the information? I don't know. If I had this parental responsibility, why wouldn't Elisabeth Major (who held all the details) give me the information? I don't know. Elisabeth Major wrote to me "You might like to raise this as an issue in court." Why did I have to? And even if I did, what then? What would they do? Give me parental responsibility again?

This issue came up in court again in front of Judge Munby on April 19th. "The learned judge hopes and expects the mother to share with the father all the information he is entitled to on the basis of having parental responsibility."

Meanwhile, the counselling that we were supposed to have at Baker and Duncan that was supposed to turn us into happy human beings who would talk to each other happily hadn't started yet. Why? Because Jan hadn't supplied her medical details, despite them being requested the previous summer. Oh well. No surprises there.

Baker and Duncan wrote in their report of April 13th 2005 that, "All reports of the contact are satisfactory and there is evidence that Sarah enjoys her contact with her father, looks forward to it and she is renewing a very positive relationship with her dad... Sarah herself speaks well of the contact time and talks to her mother openly about it at home... For her part, Miss Green has come to accept that the future will include Sarah's relationship with her father and regular contact between them. This has been something of a breakthrough, particularly as Miss Green is able to observe that Sarah benefits from the contact and that she enjoys it... Significant progress has already been made in accordance with the plan and from my point of view this has been achieved with many smiles and no tears from Sarah.

"Mr Chick is clearly impatient to move things ahead as soon as possible to overnight staying contact and to reaching a point where he and Sarah might spend prolonged periods together, for instance on short holiday trips. This is clearly a situation to be arrived at in due course."

When due course was... this was up for grabs. Despite all the reports being positive, despite everything going as well as it possibly could, the initial six contacts went up to 18 and then to 19 and 20 without changing the format. They kept making more and more contact appointments and there was no sign of things changing. I received a revised schedule that went through to mid-August 2005. No overnight stays. They said that things should go at Sarah's pace and that was fine – obviously. But how do they know what Sarah's pace is? Sarah was cool. All the reports said she was happy and enjoying it. So why weren't things going quicker? I was impatient. I wanted to move things forward. I wanted to see more of Sarah in more natural circumstances. I wanted her to have overnight stays and stuff. Imagine – being able to put her to bed and read her a bedtime story....

On April 12th something happened that had never happened before. No, it had happened before but not for what seemed like a hundred years. I saw Sarah outside the grim confines of a contact centre. Outside the bland, grey prison-like walls of the Woking and Guildford centres, outside more human nicer, but still prison-like walls Baker and Duncan's managed centre.

Sarah and I had our first contact in the real world. They tell you what you're going to be doing, where you're going to be going, you know to the park or maybe to a farm or something, and you make plans to go. You go to the centre, meet up with the supervisor and go through a few formalities. Then, instead of going through one door into the contact room, you go through another door into the fresh air. As we walked through the door, it felt like we were being let out. It's funny. I'd been outside the centre only a few minutes before but this time when I went through the door with Sarah... I just wanted to smell the air, touch the ground.

That first time we went to Sarah's local park and played on the slides and in the playground. It was fantastic to be out in the fresh air and outside those prison-like contact cen-tres. My little girl and me. Gemma came with us and, for a short period, it was just like we were a normal family. Well, normal apart from the supervisor who had to come with us everywhere.

It was beautiful, perfect, lovely, everything I'd wanted for years. Everything except one thing. When I was with Sarah, she said to me, "Don't run away with me. Mummy said you are going to run away with me."

* * * *

I understand about the supervisors and generally it's cool. The woman we've got, Tracey, is cool and doesn't get in the way too much. She's fine on that level. But it's an odd sys-tem. Baker and Duncan are obsessed with continuity and always want us to have the same supervisor. Again, fair enough. The problem is, if she can't make it, there can't be any contact. They want to keep it stable and consistent and that's fair enough, but what if she's ill? Or what if she goes on holiday? She went on holiday for a couple of weeks ear-lier in the summer of 2005 and I had no choice, but to boo my holidays for the same period. If I didn't, I'd miss the contacts when she was away and I'd miss the contacts when I was away too. That continuity is important, but is it more important than the continuity of me seeing Sarah? I don't think so.

On April 19th, Judge Munby reported that he was very pleased to note the progress being made to date and that he would wish to see progress to be made towards Sarah having staying contact with her father during the school summer holidays. He wasn't the only one. Our time together had gone up from an hour a fortnight to two hours a fortnight. A step in the right direction, but still. Things were dragging on. Sarah and I had been denied each other so long...

Who makes the decisions about the contact, whether it will increase or stay on the same level? That's between Cafcass and the Baker and Duncan expert psychiatrists.

They get together and decide that. But ever since this contact started last December 7th, there's never been any question that things haven't been perfect, that we get on perfectly. Even the Cafcass report on July 22 said: "I am very pleased with the progress the father and mother have made in working to facilitate contact for Sarah with her father... I am positive regarding the future... it is clear she [Sarah] is enjoying renewing her relationship with the father and that contact has progressed successfully."

* * * *

My relationship with Baker and Duncan was – and is – strange. I need them. I need them to say I'm being good, that I'm nice and all that. They've got the power over Sarah and me. At the same time, they often treat me like an idiot. What might seem like small things... but they're not. And they're supposed to be he experts so they should be sensitive enough to know what's small and what's not. Contacts get changed, a time here, a day there, and they let me know by e-mail. They should phone. It's more courteous and there's a chance I might not be by my computer, I might not be checking my e-mails. Things like that. Things like always taking Jan's opinion first. Whenever there's a decision to be made – when contact will be if it has to be changed – it's always her first. Like I say, a small thing but maybe not the most sensitive.

* * * *

At the time of writing, it's August 2005 and we're still under Baker and Duncan. And Sarah still hasn't been to stay here overnight. Despite Judge Munby saying in April that they should make moves to sort out overnight stays for the school summer holidays, that never happened. Why? Who can say? You ask them. Every report that's ever been done about how I am with Sarah, or how Sarah is with me... everything says the same thing. Contact is going as well as possible. They've done their contact plan which goes on till end of August – and there's still no mention of overnight stays, which he was told to do by the courts. He's being paid £10,000 to get this sorted out. Maybe they should pay him £20,000 and he might do as he's told.

*   *   *   *

Why are things dragging? You tell me. I understand that we must not rush things – of course – but it's now eight months after the first Baker and Duncan supervised contact. Eight months during which time not a negative word about any of us has been uttered. Of course, it could be argued that it's in Baker and Duncan's interests to keep things as they are. The longer we're under their watchful eye, the longer they get paid. It's the same with the solicitors. The longer they're 'representing' you, the more money they get. After a while, it's difficult to look at this whole story and see nothing but a gravy train where various bodies and people are getting rich off other people's misery. But you've got to try and put that out of your mind. You've got to stay focussed. Slowly, things are moving forward.

Happily too, Sarah's illnesses seem to have cleared up now! Between January 2002 and March 2003, she was too ill to come to contact about 20 times. But since December 2004 when Jan was advised that she could be at risk of losing residence if she kept ignoring our contact order... Sarah hasn't been ill once.

In mid-August we had our first unsupervised contact. Can you imagine that? Probably not. Me and Gemma and Sarah together alone. Just us. No contact centre. No supervisor. Nothing unnecessary. We were together from 10 in the morning till 5pm – the longest time I'd seen Sarah for four years We went to Jan's place where Tracey, our supervisor was waiting with Sarah. We picked her up and went to the seaside, then went home and dropped her off.

It was a beautiful day – in every sense. It's a strange situation, you've got to keep reminding yourself to enjoy it, to savour every minute, but the reality is that half the time you're looking at your watch, thinking, "Only three hours left..." and half the time, you're desperate not to be late on the drop off, because you know what that would mean: a black mark. When we left the beach, Sarah said, "Why we have to go now?" It killed me cos I didn't have a good answer and dads are supposed to know everything.

The best thing is that Sarah's been to my house now. Again with the supervisor, but she's cool. She just sits in the garden and reads and whatever. She leaves us alone and that's cool. What do we do here? We do the normal things parents do with their children, just the normal things - play with Barbie stickers and do up her bedroom. And it's beautiful. You know, if at that moment, someone came to the door and had a look in, they'd think we were a proper, normal family.

APPENDIX

I'm not the only one who's gone through this. I'm not the first and, chances are, I won't be the last. Hopefully the situation will change and there won't be many more fathers who find themselves in the same sort of position as I did. I spoke to many other fathers during the writing of this – some who are involved and some who aren't – and everyone I spoke to expressed a sympathetic interest.

I just wanted to include a few other stories from a few other fathers because… Well, because I want you to know that it's not just me. What happened to me isn't because I am who I am, and it didn't happen to me because of what I am. I didn't happen because I'm tall or short or thin or fat or black or white or rich or poor or anything. It happened to me because I'm a father.

Below you'll find a few stories, a few extracts, from different people I've spoken to. They're all different, but all the same underneath. There are also a couple of interviews and some notes on the Government's position. I did want to include an interview with Fathers4Justice, but they seemed reluctant to do this.

I'd like to apologise to Jonathan and the others whose stories aren't here – there's no reason other than it's very hard to put cries and sobs into words…

"I don't need to tell you my story, but just think about this. I guess it'll be mainly other fathers in my situation who are going

to read your book, and if that's the case it's a bit of a shame. The chances are they know it all anyway. But if there are any people – men or women, it doesn't matter – who are still in warm, real relationships with children and love, do one thing. Stop reading and look at your child. Take a few minutes. Now imagine that someone comes into the room and takes them away. Now read the rest of the book. Not nice, is it?"

*   *   *   *

"I'd read all the stories about Father4Justice and all those blokes and, to be honest, I was probably just the same as everyone else. You see someone who's done something wrong and you can't help but think "No smoke without fire" and there were stories in the papers about some of them that made you think "No wonder their wife left them" but then… I don't know, suddenly you end up spending the night in jail and you really start to wonder. The police knocked on my door at 6am and took me away in my dressing gown to the police station. I'm just about the most law-abiding bloke you could ever meet. I've never done anything wrong, I've never been in trouble with the law, nothing. I've got my own business and all that and everything's fine, but the fact is that I was taken to the police station at 6am in my dressing gown. And why? Because my ex-wife had phoned up and said that I was sexually abusing her. Had I? Of course not.

What had happened was that we'd split up – amicably at first – but relations between us had deteriorated. It was all about rubbish, really. Money mainly. She started making what I considered were unreasonable demands, totally going against what we'd agreed. I said "no" and that's when the problems started. Suddenly Lydia – our daughter – was ill quite a lot. Or away visiting friends. Or something. It went weeks between visits. Months. And it was all payback for me not giving in to her financial demands.

It got really messy and, in frustration, I held back the maintenance payments. Well, if she wasn't going to play the game, why should I? And that's when the police came round.

I was astounded by what they said, the idea... But I guess if you look at it from their side, they can't take any chances. Sexual abuse happens and I don't suppose there's a 'type'. But it's mad. How could it get to that stage? How can two people who once lived and loved together become like that? I suppose that's a different subject, but what really got me was that in the end it doesn't matter whose fault it is. You can spend your life arguing about who said what and who did what. What you've got to understand is that, as a man, not only is it your fault, but you're the one who's going to pay. You're the one who loses out, you're the one who is on the outside looking in. And the thing that you've got to remember is that there's nothing you can do about it."

* * * *

"I could tell you a thousand things about this but until it's you it's happening to you'll never understand. It's the little things that you can't really understand until it hits you. Small things kill you. Like for example, there always used to be cake sales at the school, just raising money for whatever. Mostly, it was a pain in the backside. You were expected to go and help out and, you know, once or twice it's fun but mostly it's a nuisance. Believe me, once it's taken away from you, you'll never see it as a nuisance again. It's those small things, the things that you don't even talk about, those are the things you miss. Everyone always talks about things like bath time and bed time and reading stories and, yeah sure, that's all important, but it's funny. It's the things you didn't want to do, the things that you couldn't be bothered with, those are the things that you miss. When you split up with your partner, you never think about stuff like that."

* * * *

"It's like you're standing on a rug and suddenly someone pulls it and… You're on your backside and you don't know how you got there. It's like one minute your head is full of useless statistics like "two in every three marriages ends in divorce" – and I don't even know if that's true. It's just something you hear – the next minute… Bang. Your life is finished. Everything you've worked for, everything you've built up… it's gone. Would I have stayed in the house if I'd have known what was going to happen? I don't know. You think to yourself that all this arguing, all this fighting, how can it do anyone any good? You think to yourself it's not doing us any good and it's not doing the kid any good. So you go, but when you make that decision you've got no idea really what you're doing. It was a nightmare before, but this is much worse, it's worse than a nightmare. If you've not been through it, you can't even imagine it. If you're sitting reading this, you can't begin to understand. Everything is taken away from you, everything. Your home, your world, it's all taken. And then when they've taken that, they take your kid too.

When it's all going wrong, when you can start to see things going pear-shaped, it's easy to get all paranoid about what's being said to your child about you. But then they take your child away and you realise that you weren't being paranoid at all."

*　　*　　*　　*

"It's difficult to say when it started. Looking back it seems that one day we were a regular family doing regular things, the next I was on the outside, looking in. It was almost like I was in a zoo, but I was the one in a cage, looking at the family walking past having fun.

All relationships struggle from time to time and ours had had its fair share of struggles. We were arguing more and more and the atmosphere in the house was getting worse and worse. Our daughter, Emma, was four-years-old and, in the toughest decision I'll ever have to make, I decided that enough was enough. My relationship had moved from being bad to being destructive and it seemed to me that the only way forward was to move out. We were to become just another statistic. But it was when I moved out that everything started to go wrong.

I was really naïve about the whole thing. I thought I'd move out and that things would basically carry on as normal, but pretty soon it became clear that it wasn't going to be that way. As soon as I was gone, it seemed that Cathy – my partner – changed personality. I can't honestly put my hand on my heart and say that when I moved out there was deep love between us, but suddenly it seemed that the opposite was true.

It started when she said things like I couldn't use the house and anything I had in the house suddenly belonged to her. Frankly I didn't care about the hoover or whatever, but it was a nuisance. I had to start from scratch in every respect. Things like my records, my books, old photograph albums... they were all gone. I couldn't get hold of any of them. Then it started with Emma.

I used to see her every weekend, but gradually that became a problem. One weekend merged into another and excuses merged into excuses.

At first we didn't have any formal arrangement – we'd always said that we could deal with it ourselves and that we didn't need solicitors – and I used to go round and see her at the weekend. I'd have an arrangement to go round and take her shopping on Saturday morning, for example, but I'd knock on the door and there'd be no one there. The next weekend it would be the same. Before I knew where I was, a month had gone by without me spending any time with Emma.

You cannot imagine the pain that this caused. The normal things that you do... suddenly it's all gone. I really don't know what caused this all to happen."

INTERVIEW
JIM PARTON - Families Need Fathers
(spokesman)

What can men do if a relationship broken down. Is there a right way and a wrong way to split up?
Of course there is. Ideally the couple split up in an amicable and co-operative manner. But we all know that isn't always the way. And it only takes one of the couple to wreck that as an outcome

Is the result cut and dried? The woman has the power the man doesn't?
No, it's not totally cut and dried. If you manage your case well from the outset then you've got a chance as a man. Once you're on the defensive, it's very, very difficult to retrieve the situation, but at the outset it's possible to fix it so that that doesn't happen.

Are there two or three basic things that a man should do?
The most important thing is this. What a lot of men do is wait for 'it' to happen. They should take the initiative. If they can see that their relationship is going pear-shaped, they should try to be the one who, if it's going to go that way, puts the application into court rather than waiting for the other side to do it. Then they'll be on the defensive from thereon in.

Application for?
For contact, for residence, for whatever outcome the guy wants.

They should be more pro-active?
Yes. What happens very often is that the man assumes he is going to lose and waits for the thing to get to court and then rolls over. And then if his partner starts to break contact orders or agreements, it's very difficult for him to get the whole thing re-established.

Does this means that whoever goes on the offensive first is better placed?
I think it probably does mean that, yes.

And does that not play into the hands of the adversarial system?
Totally, yes. I do think, though, that if you go first it does make a big difference. There is still a big bias in favour of women, but you can reduce that by going into court first.

How does that bias manifest itself?
The societal expectation is reflected in the way that judges decide things. There's still a perception that looking after kids is women's work, and going out to work is Dad's work.

Isn't that an old fashion view, a view that's not relevant to now?
I agree. But moves are being made to change it. There's a pull from two directions: you've got firstly feminists who want equality ion the workplace and if there's going to be equality in the workplace there's got to equality at home too. Women will have to stop being the bosses at home, and it could just as easily be the man who looks after the children if it's the woman who has the greater earning potential. So you've got feminists pulling on one side and on the other side you've got fathers saying we want equality too.

Is it getting better?
I don't know that it is. We still see horrendous cases where blokes have done nothing wrong and still can't see their kids. We still plenty of that.

You talk about feminism and gender equality. Let's assume that most judges are male.
Well, yes. They're not feminists, but they don't side with the men if you like because they want to look after the ladies.

That sounds ridiculous.
Yes, but it's a natural male instinct. I'll talk about equality between the genders but I'll still open doors for women. You've got to be a bit realistic. Men are not going to morph into women and women are not going to morph in to men. It's just not going to happen.

Is there a particular outcome you want to see?
We want to see shared parenting after a separation. An awful lot of people are excluded from seeing their children for no very good reason. Being a good father rather than a superb father often isn't good enough. I think good enough fathers should be allowed to see their kids. Once you get into that adversarial situation you can say all sorts of things about anyone. Even me.

Can you be seen as a good father?
No, that's the biggest problem. Once you get into that contact situation you're always walking on eggshells, you can't be natural. You've got to be on time, there on time. You're constantly looking at the clock. And you might have different ideas about parenting, so what you consider to be the right thing to do – for example, how much television you allow the child to watch, or what time they should go to bed, might be seen as an example of you being a bad parent. So you can't be that very good dad figure, you can only be

rather artificial and a very anxious person. So when we say we want a 50/50 split, it's not necessarily time we're talking about, it's about sharing power so that you're no longer walking on those eggshells and blokes can be confident about their parenting and he's not constantly being scrutinised about his parenting style.

INTERVIEW

ALAN CRITCHLEY – Regional Director, Cafcass
(the Children and Families Court Advisory and Support Service), Eastern Region

What can a parent expect from Cafcass?

People come to us and ask, 'What can I expect from Cafcass?' which is an entirely reasonable question. Can I expect half the holidays and every other weekend and a visit in midweek? - a very common format. And what we'll do is say, 'Well, no you can't expect that. Let's talk to you, let's talk to the child's mother, lets' talk to the children and we'll work it out on an individual basis.' Each child and each situation is different. But what that leads to is people saying to us 'You're not being transparent with me. I don't know what I'm going to get' and already they're on the back foot because there's a perception that we're against fathers and it can lead to some difficult discussions at an early stage.

There are difficulties within the family system that we would acknowledge and it's our role to do something about that. Because the system is pretty slow, because the system is pretty adversarial, one of the big problems is that what tends to happen is that when people split it tends to be the man who moves out. One can ask why this happens but it is what tends to happen.

What then happens is that the man can lose contact on a temporary basis. For example, say there is a lot of anger, say

214

there is no intermediary, say the father has nowhere to live at that point, what's a typical scenario is that mother will say 'Okay, you get yourself somewhere and we can start having contact'. The father then goes off and gets a flat, a process that can take some time. He comes back and says I've got a flat and I want to start having contact. The mother may well be angry about all sorts of things and she might well say, 'Look you haven't seen him for two or three months and he's very cross with you for walking out.'

She might say you can see him for an hour here or there, she might say you're not going to see him at all until you start paying me lots of money and use the money as a weapon

By what right can she do this?
None. Parents are gender-neutral in the law.

And in reality?
In reality what often happens is that father has gone for some reason. Mother is left with child and may be very angry with the father and the child is picking this up. The mother may be displaying her anger openly in front of the child, saying things like 'Oh, that father of yours, I always knew he'd leave...' or whatever. The child picks up the message that the father is bad news. So when the father says that he wants to see the child, she then says 'Well, he doesn't want to see you'. And so we get into that difficult situation. And that tends to be how it happens. So when you talk about the mother being favoured by the system, you must understand we're working in some very difficult areas that are difficult to untangle.

What's the best tactic for a father in that situation?
Our viewpoint is that a child needs both parents, but by the time we get involved we're at least a month, more like two months down the line by which time the status quo has been

established and it's very difficult to get out of.

The best tactic for the father is that although he might move out of the family home and take himself away from that domestic situation, he must keep as much contact with the child at all times. Absolutely.

Things can get worse as time develops. Another familiar scenario is that father moves out, gets himself somewhere else and contact is happening quite well. Father gets himself another partner and mother might well say 'well I'm not having him seeing your new partner. I'm certainly not having him staying there'.

In all these scenarios, the child gets used like a tennis ball.
The compounding factor is that what we're dealing with are these human emotions like love that turns to hate and how powerful is that?

Children haven't got the emotional development to deal with all this.
Of course not. One of the things that we are constantly saying is that children are – or can be abused – and are – or can be- very distressed by these proceedings. Older children can show higher levels of distress because they tend to act as a support for their resident carer back at home and sometimes by the time the parent has moved on, the children haven't. They are still feeling responsible, still picking up the pieces.

Not only from the child's point of view is it better to keep contact going but – and this applies to both parents – it's best not to show the child their own anxieties and emotions. The last thing that any child wants is tearful father knocking on the door saying 'I need you. I want you' because that's just more emotional overload. The father, no matter how he's feeling, needs to be as cool and supportive as that child needs. It's really difficult stuff.

Do you think Cafcass is unfairly criticised?
I think there's a perception problem. As recently as the late 1990s, we were criticised by some women's groups who used to feel we encouraged too much contact with fathers. And we still get criticised by women's groups - but not as publicly. In 2005, there was publicity by Women's Aid about the number of children who have died or been injured during contact visits. So there are quite powerful arguments on both sides – and need to risk assess the situation.

How do you make judgements?
With enormous difficulty.

Does the court system work?
Once you get into the 10% who go to court the system doesn't work very well. It's slow. It's adversarial. Often what happens when people separate is that they will go and see their solicitor and solicitors don't always work in the best interests of the child. Solicitors can be working in the best interests of their clients - which could be about money. Once you get into the court system a lot of the proceedings concentrate on previous claims in terms of "She said that to me" and "He did that to me" and then it's about proving. Did you really say that to her, did she really do that to him? And it shouldn't be about that. It should be about children and what's best for the child.

Then, court orders often don't work because there isn't much you can do to enforce a court order at the moment. In theory prison could be used, but if you were a judge would you send the resident parent to prison? For very good reasons, judges don't like doing it.

If a judge makes a ruling that contact has to take place and it doesn't, could the judge not simply change resident parent?
A not-uncommon scenario. Yes, you could change residents,

and I've seen that happen. But if they say contact should happen and it doesn't and the child has grown up in effect not knowing the father, you're not going to change resident parent because the child has no relationship with that father. In effect the child doesn't know the father.

What you don't do is take a five or six year old child away from a mother and given them to a man who, in effect, they don't know. What you might do is give her to foster parents.

There must be a degree of looking at him and his circumstances.
Yes, of course you do all that, but it's still scary stuff because if the mother's been saying to the child since that child was a dot that their father's not a nice man, that he's a scary man, that he wants to harm the or whatever....

What abut the idea of a 50/50 split?
Some of the groups say that they want a 50/50 split, that each partner has the child 50% of the time. What we would say is that that doesn't work for children. It needs to be a different arrangement for each child. Depending on things like geography, or hostility between the parents. Sometimes handover is a very fraught time.

Has the rise of the fathers groups made any impact, positive or otherwise?
I think it has. It's certainly raised media awareness of this whole complex area; it's also raised the confidence of fathers. It's all about the idea of increasing the importance of fathers and increasing the importance of a father in a child's life. That's beginning to happen more and more

Do you think people didn't really take on the role of fathers?
I think it's been a general trend. How many years ago was it that the father wasn't involved in the birth of the child?

What we're seeing now – and it's not just in the legal bit – is an increase in the role of the fathers, generally. And it's becoming more acceptable for fathers to stay at home while mothers go out to work. That kind of general change is happening.

Have the father's groups a catalyst for that awareness?
In terms of the legal situation, they have. I think it was happening anyway. But in terms of the media it's highlighted some issues. I'm not sure that their tactics were right and I think that now Fathers4Justice are talking about having a parliamentary lobbyist, which may be the best way forward.

If they are changing attitudes so fundamentally, should we view these fathers in a similar light to, say, suffragettes? Should we see them as Pankhurst figures? Would that be a correct historical judgement?
I'm not sure about that. But there is going to reform and the father's group movement – and the attendant media hype – has given it a real impetus.

In January 2005, the Government published:
"Parental Separation: Children's Needs and Parents' Responsibilities: Next Steps"

This is an advisory paper that followed the launch of the Green Paper *"Parental Separation: Children's Needs and Parents' Responsibilities in July 2004"*.

It is available, free of charge, at http://www.dfes.gov.uk/ childrensneeds/docs/ParentalSeparation.pdf

In response to this, Cafcass issued the following:

CAFCASS Developments

CAFCASS accepts that the present way of working in private law does not provide the best possible service for children and families. In particular, the adversarial system mitigates against encouraging agreements, there are systemic delays which can lead to an established status quo which is then difficult to shift, Welfare Reports can highlight previous difficulties rather than encourage child focused parenting, there is an inconsistency of approach by CAFCASS and others across the country and there is a difficulty in enforcing court orders.

CAFCASS starts from the position that fathers and mothers are equally important to children. Furthermore CAFCASS believes that a child should have good and meaningful contact with both parents. This contact will normally be of sufficient duration to allow the parent to play a full part in the life of the child. The only exception to direct and unsupervised contact would be where a child may suffer harm from one parent. In each case these exceptions will be assessed and will probably be referred to another agency.

CAFCASS particularly welcomes the Private Law Programme and Next Steps and intends to respond to the individual components as follows:

- Pre-court: CAFCASS has begun to work with others in local communities to provide information about where to seek help in a way that will achieve good results for children without resort to court proceedings.

- Court: CAFCASS is in the process of agreeing and developing Dispute Resolution schemes in all Family Courts with agreed national criteria. We aim to have these in place by March 2006. The aim is to achieve an agreement that is in the best interests of the child or children with minimal delay.
- Where satisfactory agreement is not achieved at Dispute Resolution stage and CAFCASS has a role we will work to whatever timescale the needs of the case determine. If the case is a difficult and complex one it may take a few months, if it is relatively simple it may be a matter of days or weeks. We will move away from the "one size fits all" approach of a welfare report taking twelve weeks.
- We will move towards continuity with Family Court Advisers. Likewise the DCA is moving towards judicial continuity. In this way the Family Court Adviser and the judge will be familiar with the issues and will be able to work closely together to ensure that the best possible resolution for the child will be achieved.
- After a hearing: CAFCASS intends to be able to offer post-order follow up in exceptional cases. Currently if the conditions of an order have not been kept the mother or father has to return the case to court. This takes time, increases delay and may well increase the level of hostility. When post-order follow up begins CAFCASS will, for example, contact both parents on a Monday to ask whether contact happened at the weekend as set out in the court order. If it didn't CAFCASS will inform the court and the case will be returned quickly to court and heard by the judge who made the order. In this way swift action can be taken to ensure that orders are complied with. CAFCASS

is working through the practicalities and budgetary implications of this and will update service user groups when a timescale becomes clearer.

- Family Assistance Orders are currently available and about 500 a year are made. The nature of these is likely to be altered with the time limit extended to one year and the necessity for parental consent removed. We intend to use these orders creatively and constructively to achieve better outcomes for children. Again, we will update service user groups when we are clearer with regard to this.

- 9.5 representation: CAFCASS is currently involved in approximately 1500 of these cases across the country. The CAFCASS Family Court Adviser represents the child who is made a "party" to the case. Managing a case this way can be very effective where there is a high level of animosity between the parents.

We do believe that the sum total of the changes in the Private Law Programme and Next Steps will make a profound difference to the Family Justice system and will provide better outcomes for children.

This is a busy and fast moving time in the Family Justice System. CAFCASS is very keen to work with statutory and voluntary organisations so that we all work towards creating the best possible system for children and families. We are committed to collaborative working and learning from each other.

Me and my daughter
The Guildford contact centre in 2002

Before the split
July 2001
On holiday in Devon.

Me, my daughter and Marvin December 2001.
The last contact,
outside of a contact centre,
for three years.

My daughter in the nursery playground July 2004,
My first glimpse of her for three months

An example of the 'contact' I had
for 21 months despite the contact order at this time.

the ex of mine if, the first time she failed to show up for a contact – Sarah's ill – she had a subpoena slapped on her head? That would have been the end of that wand this would have been a very short book. In fact, I wouldn't have had to write it.

After three years we were given a Cafcass legal officer, Elisabeth Major, rather than a normal run-of-the-mill Cafcass officer. Maybe it's because we've gone from the Family Court to the High Court. (Elisabeth Major was supposed to be Sarah's 'guardian'. Excuse me, I thought I was Sarah's guardian? Oh well.) Now that we're a high profile story they need a high profile person in charge. Somehow by going up a crane I became a more important person and they were concerned that I keep quiet. But they knew what to do to keep me quiet – just do right by me and my daughter, but they didn't do that. They thought they could get away with what they did in the secret Family Courts. But I am one person whose child they shouldn't nick because I was going to come after them. The Royal Courts Of Injustice is still held behind closed doors. It's the same as the old Family Courts. A more impressive building but the same old secrets.

She was supposed to be an expert, so I decided to give her the benefit of the doubt because, well, you've got to. If something new comes along you've got to give it a chance. But at the same time I knew that however good or whatever this legal officer was, the chances that they'd turn round and say that Cafcass has been incompetent and corrupt... It's not going to happen. Still, if she really is an expert, she'll soon realise what's been going on in this case. She'll soon see.

If Elisabeth Major really was an expert, she must have come across these stories before. She must have come across people behaving like this before. It's inconceivable that she hadn't seen the tricks and games. But they truth is that these people don't give a toss. They say they do, but they don't. One minute they're saying: "Mr Chick's commitment to his daughter cannot be questioned," that I'm the best dad in the world, but at the same time they're not seeing things that are staring them in the face. And what "she (the mother) says" always overrides factual things that are indisputable and are staring them in the face.

At the next contact hearing at the Royal Courts Of Justice on July 28, we got Judge Munby. Now he was supposed to be a top man so I thought maybe I'd have a chance of something proper. Some chance. He'd made a bit of a name amongst the disaffected fathers groups after writing in April 2004 about another case he was ruling on: "From the father's perspective the last two years of the litigation have been an exercise in absolute futility. When his counsel told me that the father felt very let down by the system, I was not surprised. I can understand why he expresses that view. He has every right to express that view. In a sense it is shaming to have to say it, but I personally agree with his view. It is very, very disheartening."

Elisabeth Major reported (on July 2nd) and said that because Sarah and I had been apart for so long, we should be referred to a specialist agency, Baker and Duncan, for assessment. Baker and Duncan Family Consultancy, to give them their full title, are a firm of expert child psychiatrists who specialise in cases like ours where's there's been a major gap in the contact and where everyone might need a bit of expert advice in the early stages. It's only a small firm, but they're supposed to be the top people. It was something. Then, in the recommendations part of her report, it said "In the meantime, the order for contact dated December 18, 2002, be suspended".

Judge Munby agreed and ordered "contact be suspended". Great. It was 16 months after Jan had unofficially suspended contact and here was the court making it official. I understood that their reasoning, that it had been so long since Sarah and I had seen each other that we needed assistance to re-start our relationship when we got back to-